ADVENTURES IN
URBAN FOOD GROWING

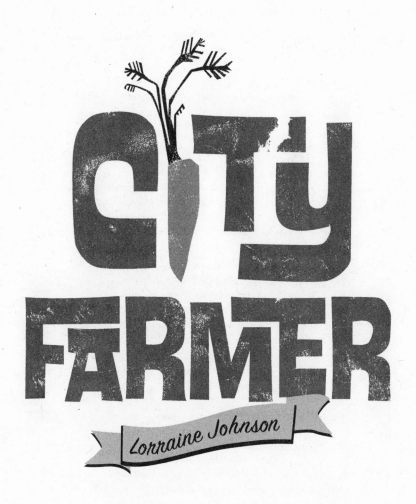

CITY FARMER

Lorraine Johnson

GREYSTONE BOOKS

D&M PUBLISHERS INC.

Vancouver/Toronto/Berkeley

For Michael Levenston, Canada's unofficial
minister of urban agriculture for more than thirty years

. . . . .

Greystone Books
An imprint of D&M Publishers Inc.
2323 Quebec Street, Suite 201
Vancouver BC Canada V5T 4S7
www.greystonebooks.com

Cataloging data available from Library and Archives Canada
ISBN 978-1-55365-519-0 (pbk.)
ISBN 978-1-55365-628-9 (ebook)

Editing by Susan Folkins
Cover and text design by Naomi MacDougall
Cover city illustration © CSA Snapstock Illustration/Veer
Printed and bound in Canada by Friesens
Text printed on acid-free, FSC-certified paper that is forest friendly
(100% post-consumer recycled paper) and has been processed chlorine free
Distributed in the U.S. by Publishers Group West

We gratefully acknowledge the financial support of the Canada Council
for the Arts, the British Columbia Arts Council, the Province of British
Columbia through the Book Publishing Tax Credit, and the Government of Canada
through the Canada Book Fund for our publishing activities.

Mixed Sources
Cert no. SW-COC-001271
© 1996 FSC
FSC

Contents

. . .

INTRODUCTION: Bringing Dinner Home · 1

1 Sowing the City, Reaping the Benefits · 9

2 Embracing a Food-growing Ethic · 31

3 Productive Possibility · 47

4 Harvesting Space · 67

5 Rethinking Convention: *Finding Soil and Sites* · 91

6 Lessons of Care: *Food Gardens as Nurturing Hubs* · 119

7 People Power: *Growing Together in Community Gardens* · 131

8 Rogues on a Mission: *Guerrilla Gardening and Foraging* · 155

9 What the Cluck?: *Backyard Chickens* · 179

10 The Edible City · 203

EPILOGUE: Adventures in Possibility · 215

RESOURCES
*A Selected List of Urban Farms and
Edible Demonstration Gardens* · 221

*A Selected List of Urban Agriculture
and Food-related Organizations* · 229

A Selected List of Books · 233

ACKNOWLEDGMENTS · 243

INDEX · 245

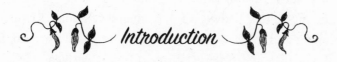

Introduction

· · ·

BRINGING DINNER HOME

MY NEPHEW CHRISTOPHER, ten at the time, had never seen a real live pea. Or even a recently alive pea. The weird pod-thing I had in my hand, shelling as we talked, completely mystified him. "What's that?" he finally asked, with a bit of my-aunt-always-does-strange-stuff in his voice. "It's a pea!" I exclaimed, not hiding my surprise. (As a non-parent, I didn't get the memo about feigning nonchalance at questions that shock.) He chewed over my answer for a long time, and then said, full of satisfaction, "Ahh, peas in a pod—now I get it."

The phrase may have finally made sense to him, but the lesson was incomplete without a taste. "Would you like to try one?" I offered. "Umm, I don't like peas," he mumbled, echoing ten-year-old boys everywhere. "Oh come on, just try it," I said. And so he popped it in his mouth to humor his odd aunt, and as he munched, his face changed from anticipatory yuck to something approaching pleasure. "It's sweet, not mushy," he enthused, "not like canned peas." I offered him another. Pretty soon we were shelling at a great rate, stuffing little peas in our faces, talking with our mouths full. It felt like a minor triumph, winning this pea convert through direct contact with something so recently attached to a stem.

Our day together had been full of such revelations. My nephew Christopher and niece Deanna were visiting me in Toronto, from their home in small-town Michigan. ("We live near Hell," the kids love to say, delighting in the license to swear that the name of a neighboring town provides.) Their oak-wooded community, bordering a small lake, is much like middle-class small towns throughout North America. It has large but not ostentatious homes with long driveways (some containing boats or snowmobiles). And almost every home has an acre-sized lawn with an automatic sprinkler system, a flower bed tight to the wall, and shrubs and trees dotted along the property lines.

When they come to see me in Toronto, my niece and nephew must feel that they've come not just to another country but to another planet. Everything about the big city delights, dazzles, and intrigues them. I usually agonize over how to amuse my young relatives (in fear of being boring and too adult), then quickly calm down when I realize that just exploring the city is amusement enough for two curious and engaged kids. We can sit for an hour in the local Coffee Time and they'll be happy with the parade of urban surprises; it was the first place they saw a man dressed as a woman.

For this visit, though, we decided to venture farther down the road with a streetcar ride (their first) to Kensington Market—a chaotic and historic outpost of multicultural urban liveliness in the center of the city, where ramshackle buildings house vegetable stands, fish shops, butchers, dry goods suppliers, and second-hand clothing stores. My niece and nephew's eyes got wider and wider as we passed a derelict parked car—a Kensington Market landmark—that the group Streets Are For People had turned into a public art piece, planting the hood with herbs, the trunk with trees, and the open roof with lawn grass. The bumper sticker read "Parks not Parking" and the graffiti on the doors "Community Vehicular Reclamation Project." I doubt that the kids had ever seen such a creative compost bin—the *inside* of a car.

We wove through sidewalks crowded with tattooed, pierced punks and old market shopkeepers barking directions at delivery truck drivers. We dodged stalls overflowing with produce. We ducked under dried fish hanging from rafters. We walked around jumbled café chairs with buskers holding court. And with each moment of increasing stimulation, my niece and nephew drank it all in, the random and unpredictable *aliveness* of it all. "They're selling food on the sidewalk!" said my nephew with disbelief, no doubt thinking of trips to the grocery store where everything edible comes securely wrapped in plastic.

This was food as they'd never seen it before. This was close contact. Peas in a pod.

WHEN EXACTLY DID we become so removed from the source of our sustenance, a disconnect that reached an extreme expression in my nephew's bollixed reaction to fresh peas? For my generation (a demographic cohort that entered the world in the 1960s, shaped and solidified our habits and patterns in the '70s, and stumbled into independence in the '80s), I blame the astronauts. Okay, maybe not each one personally, but the whole space program. This was the miraculous, mind-bending, perspective-exploding, boundary-busting leap into the unknown that not only brought us a new conception of our planet and our place, but also launched Tang into popularity. Perhaps you remember the stuff? It was the

3

"drink of the astronauts"—juice that came not from the messy pulp of oranges but from pouches of "flavor crystals." In much the same way that K-Tel's Patty Stacker (in those late-night television ads for the gadget, which shaped ground hamburger into perfectly stackable rounds) promised that "your hands need never touch the meat," Tang offered a fruit drink whose relationship with actual, *touched* fruit was about as distant as the moon. We drank it by the gallon, vicariously thrilling to the modern out-there-ness of it all. How convenient it was to reconstitute food—from a *bag*.

The antiseptic compression of edibility that is Tang couldn't be any further from real food if we tried. Real food carries its dirt along with it, no matter how hard we scrub. Soil memory lurks in the folds and wrinkles and even in the smooth skins of fruits and vegetables, giving them their character and their flavor. The French call this *terroir,* and while the term is mainly deployed for wine (*bien sur,* the idea comes from French food culture, after all) it applies equally well to everything edible. Flavor and identity come from place, ineluctably and inevitably.

But how often do we put that idea on our plate and eat it? Not very. Our dinner tables sag under the weight of food trucked, flown, trained, and otherwise transported across the globe. Estimates vary, but the standard statistic for the average distance traveled by the food we eat is 1,500 miles. Our dinners are often more globe-trotting, more worldly, than we are.

If our taste buds demand raspberries in February, artichokes in December, and corn on the cob in March, global agricultural production feeds our seasonally jumbled desires as quickly as you can say greenhouse gas emissions. And *that* is what we're producing and consuming with each forkful. Well, that and six-syllable chemicals banned in North America, plus labor practices that would put us to shame if we took more time to consider them.

In short, we eat in ignorance of what our food costs us, costs others, and costs the earth.

It doesn't have to be this way, and increasingly it's not. In the past few years there has been a groundswell—is revolution too dramatic a word?—of interest in where our food comes from, how our food choices affect the world, and what we might do to create a saner, healthier, fairer, safer, and greener food system. The fact that all of these er's add up to tastier food is icing on the quintuple-layer cake.

Getting closer to our food—becoming eaters who are deeply, intimately, connected with what we eat—necessarily involves learning more of the details of its production. Even if we're not the ones actually growing the beets or nurturing the chickens, the more we know of the work involved, all the how's, where's, why's, what's, and when's that collide to create sustenance, the better able we'll be to make informed decisions about how we sustain ourselves. And when that production occurs near where the majority of us spend our lives, in cities, the better chance we have of seeing, learning, knowing, or at least being somewhat curious about, those details.

Of course, people have been growing food in cities for millennia. The residents of the world's first cities raised vegetables, fruits, livestock, and grains in close proximity to their homes. Urban agriculture is as ancient a practice as gathering together to live in urban communities. Yet as Brian Halweil points out in his book *Eat Here,* "a range of forces in the modern era—the industrial revolution, the evolution of the megacity, the invention of refrigeration—helped to render urban farming obsolete ... The engines of modern civilization began to squeeze farming out of cities."

While few feel nostalgic for the pre-industrialized city (I, for one, love my refrigerator, and I know my grandmother said a prayer of thanks every time she turned on the water tap), an impulse deeper than romantic wistfulness now leads us to reflect on what we lost when food production was squeezed out of our lives. My generation is probably the most de-skilled in all of history in terms of knowing about the basic practices of food production: saving seeds, planting seeds, nurturing and growing plants. In other words, out of sight can lead to out of mind, which in turn can lead to the defeated attitude of "well, that's just the way things are, isn't it?" It's not much of a leap to say that such an attitude can lead to flavorless tomatoes, hard as rocks, grown halfway around the globe and delivered to us as grim industrial offerings—not food.

THERE ARE, NO doubt, huge problems with every aspect of our food system, from the seeds planted (for the most part, corporately controlled seeds that are chosen for industrial efficiency instead of flavor, nutrition, and diversity), through to growing methods that deplete or contaminate air, water, and soil, to distribution and retailing that favor global over local priorities and thus allow us to download true costs (in carbon emissions, in pollution, in waste) to the future. Transforming this skewed infrastructure is necessary work that could consume a lifetime—if indeed we had the luxury of such a slow pace. Many have argued that we don't.

In the face of this enormous challenge, planting a food garden might seem like an act of miniscule proportion, laughably obscure in the grand scheme, the equivalent of fiddling (or hoeing) while Rome burns. But hope is the defining and guiding force that sends shovels into soil. We garden for the future. And what is hope if not nourishment for an idea of what the future might be?

This is a lot of symbolic weight for a radish to carry. Especially a radish grown in the city, a place where food gardens are usually conceived of as products of hobby and leisure, not as things of necessity. But more and more North Americans—80 percent of whom live in urban areas—are looking at the broken food system and instead of throwing down forks in despair, or gagging on dinner, they are planting edible gardens. Some are doing it for the simple pleasures of productivity; others are making more declarative political, social, cultural, and economic statements. All are participating in a transformative gesture toward a different future.

Even when we take small steps to gain control of what we eat, we know that these acts are neither the whole answer nor are they possible for everyone. But each carrot grown, each backyard egg collected, each community plot tended, and each rooftop tomato plucked is fertile nourishment for the growing revolution that's changing our relationship with food.

And connection with food doesn't get much closer than hands in the dirt.

one

SOWING THE CITY,
REAPING THE BENEFITS

AS A YOUNG child growing up in the small southwestern Ontario city of Galt, I wanted to hide my family's vegetable garden, pretend it didn't exist, erase it from the neighborhood. I felt embarrassed by our rows of beans, peas, tomatoes, and strawberries. They were like a banner announcing our less-than-robust financial circumstances to the community. Everyone else seemed to be straining for the upmarket trappings of consumer culture—buying glamorous cars like convertibles while we made do with a Rambler station wagon; eating exotic fare like avocadoes while we had pigs' tails for dinner. And growing food was a decidedly down-market thing to do. Our garden signaled need, just one more item in the long list of evidence that my family did not fit in. It didn't help that, one year, during a period of compost experimentation, my father buried food waste directly in the soil between the rows. After a particularly heavy rain, egg shells started poking up through the dirt. Yet another advertisement for our oddness.

I remember the precise moment when my feelings about the garden began to change from embarrassment to engagement. It was after a summer dinner, when I was six. For dessert we'd had watermelon and I'd hoarded the seeds. After dinner, I sprang up from the table with the stash in my hand and a vision in my head: I was going to plant those pips. I was going to have my own little garden, tucked under the shrubs by the side of the house.

I don't know how long it took for me to realize that nothing was going to come of my plantation, that shade equals watermelon failure, that late summer is not the time to seed an annual crop in southern Ontario. But I can still summon the yearning stretch of my dreamy plan, the way it fired me up with hope for a future that included a small corner of my own tending.

I AM GLAD that I learned early on about the rhythms of food production and connection with the soil. I see so much of my adult self nascent in my childhood excitement and yearning for seasonal progression. Shelling fresh peas was an event I longed for. Hulling strawberries was a labor that made me happy. Cutting beans for the pot felt good. And eating my father's homegrown tomatoes was best of all: summer meals involved jostling with my younger sisters to be first in line for the big spoonful of seeds my father separated out from the slices. He salted the slices just right, and we couldn't wait to eat the seedy slurry that he found hard to digest.

I wonder what it's like to grow up without growing things, without connecting your food to a particular time and place and to your own labor. Perhaps because my family had that tradition, motivated by frugality, I carried it with me into adulthood through a series of apartments and houses. However unlikely the circumstances, I always managed to make room where I lived for even just a few pots of edible plants. Roommates cast dubious glances at the buckets of basil sunning on the roof and were otherwise engaged when it came time for the dangerous and daily acrobatics of rooftop watering. But they lined up when it came time for pesto suppers. I also lugged deep plastic trays (okay, I confess, they were unused cat litter trays) to balcony corners and planted them with radishes. One year, I "borrowed" the backyard of a friend's rented house and carried shovels and hoes across town on my bike, all in an effort to turn a neglected lawn into a food garden. Another year, I accepted an offer to babysit a friend's allotment garden. Squatting her plot, I invented a whole new way to grow tomatoes: letting the weeds grow high so they served as no-fuss tomato stakes. Later still, when I owned my own bit of city land and had filled that up with lettuce and bean plants, I continued to colonize any empty backyard space that friends and family would allow me, even going so far as to plant watermelons and blackberry canes 40 miles away, in another city.

In short, I've always been on the lookout for productive space—anywhere, anybody's—to enlist in the adventure of growing at least some of my food. (Luckily, most of my adventures have turned out better than my watermelon plantation did.)

HOWEVER SMALL MY tentative gestures might have been, they participate in a much larger story—a story that is chipping away at convention and inverting notions we've held dear for decades. Food comes from farms, we're told, farms that exist in the countryside, separated from cities not just by physical distance but by an attitudinal divide that is much harder to breach. The countryside is "clean" and pure, close to nature. Cities are "dirty," far from nature, essentially nature corrupted. Urban soils and air are contaminated; vandals lurk around every corner . . . And even if we could overcome these dangers, there's simply not enough room

11

in North American cities to "waste" space doing something that properly belongs in the country. So the old story goes, anyway.

But when we dig in the dirt and cultivate food, what we're also doing—beyond growing the basil—is staking out territory for an expanded notion of what our cities might be. We're making room for productivity in a place defined for too long as incapable of meeting, even partially, one of our most basic needs.

Maybe this explains, to some degree at least, the giddy high that comes from unearthing an urban potato. Yes, it's most definitely *just* a potato, and that is reason enough for deep satisfaction (for those of us who love the lowly spud). But it's also a *possibility*—of a different way of living in cities.

Given the heightened interest in urban food production, one could be forgiven for thinking that to live a virtuous life now requires that we garden 24/7. If we're not hoeing, seeding, weeding, watering, harvesting, canning, and otherwise preserving the mountains of food necessary to sustain us through a year of eating, are we not shirking duty? No, we're living our lives and making choices that are dictated by a whole host of complex circumstances. So, let's dispense with the should's and imagine, instead, the could's. Could I plant a few pots of cucumbers, herbs, and tomatoes on my balcony? Could I do with a bit less lawn and a few more veggies? Could I plant an edible fruit tree on the boulevard? Could I grow beans up my apartment building's wall? In our answers to these questions, some of us might find a small sliver of do-ability. Others might find an obsessional pursuit that keeps us busy for the whole growing season. There's a lot of room in between.

The benefits accrue, whatever the scale. First and foremost, of course, is flavor. Ask any gardener why they're growing their own veggies and chances are that superior taste will be at or near the top of their list. Ask an industrial agronomist, on the other hand, why they've chosen a particular variety of tomato, for example, to grow by the acre-ful, and flavor rarely rates a mention. Thomas Pawlick tried this experiment. In his book *The End of Food,* he recounts his conversations with tomato-breeding experts and industry spokespeople, discussions in which he asked them what characteristics were most important in the top fifteen tomato varieties in their markets. The experts mentioned yield, size, firmness, resistance to disease, heat tolerance, uniformity of shape, and uniformity in time of ripening. Pawlick gave them a chance to add the obvious, but no one bit. As he writes, "No one mentioned the two characteristics that any ordinary consumer would likely put at the top of his or her list, namely: flavor and nutritional content. They were simply *not there,* not important, not even worth mentioning."

Industrial agriculture cares not one bit for our taste buds. And it would hardly matter if flavor *were* a top priority of the agricultural giants, because every aspect of the industrial food system works against it. From harvesting machines that demand uniform unripeness to storage methods that do ripening work best left to the sun, to the final indignity of time spent in transport trucks, flavor is diminished every step of the way.

Try this: bite into a ripe tomato just picked from the vine. Let the juice run... Freshness—taste's twin—is what we're guaranteed when we eat food straight from the plant. Even if it's not the best green pepper ever (though how often have you heard a gardener say that what they've grown is not delicious?), it is certainly the freshest ever. There are no other food-chain shortcuts we can take (even buying directly from farms or shopping at farmers' markets, for example, valuable as those are) that reduce the harvest-to-dinner distance, in time, to mere minutes. (Some gardeners take this to extremes. I have a friend who will only eat corn that is picked just as the pot on the stove hits the boil.)

13

As to what effect industrial growing methods have on nutrition, Thomas Pawlick also presents some disturbing data based on his investigations into the United States Department of Agriculture (USDA) "food tables," which measure the nutritional content of various foods. Comparing recent measures of nutritional value with figures from roughly fifty years ago, Pawlick itemizes one staggering loss of nutritional goodness after another: 30.7 percent less vitamin A in today's fresh tomatoes compared with those of 1963; a 57 percent decrease in vitamin C in potatoes; 45 percent less vitamin C in broccoli. His conclusion: "for the past 50 years the nutrients have been leaching out of nearly everything we eat . . ."

If homegrown food provides us with an instant wake-up call in flavor and freshness, and takes us outside of an industrial system that is depleting our food's nutritional value, it likewise increases our chances of conscious consumption. There are deeply political dimensions to this issue, and I'll turn to those later, but the awareness I'm referring to here is of a much more personal nature. It seems to me that one of the most meaningful gifts we receive from the food we grow ourselves is the gift of story. What we consume with each bite are the narratives embedded in the fruits of our labor. These stories emerge from the struggles (the squirrels or the mysterious fungus or the munching insect or whatever); the successes (the tricks to increase yield, the weeding that works); the surprises (the plant that survives neglect, the eggplant flowers that are as beautiful as any prized ornamental), and the triumphs (the cabbages bigger than the biggest of human heads). The food we grow ourselves is invested with dozens of daily dramas that give it a flavor and a meaning more enriching than anything we can buy. Our gardens are narrative forms of self expression that reveal our tastes and desires, our particular histories, who we are and how we want to create a place for ourselves in the world.

Of course, these stories, while deeply personal, are also the same stories that people have been telling for millennia. Try saying the words *to reap* and *to sow* with a straight face, and not at church. It's hard, isn't it? But these ancient words, and these ancient acts, connect our stories across time. That may sound like a heavy historical weight for a little plot of salad greens to carry, but as you pick the slugs off the lettuce and later tell the story of the slippery guck they left on your fingers, you can be sure that the trail oozes back a very long time.

It was a melon that brought this historical and narrative dimension home, most powerfully, for me. A dear friend is involved with the Cantaloupe Garden, a collective garden in Montreal. I'd always found the name charming and evocative, but didn't give it much thought until I found out that growing in the Cantaloupe Garden is a particular melon variety called the Montreal Melon that dates back to the French settlers of the seventeenth century. This is truly a melon with a capital-H History, and stories galore. Grown on the island of Montreal since the late 1600s, this enormous melon—it can reach 20 pounds or more—was once so popular (the melon's green flesh carries a hint of nutmeg) that by the late 1800s it was one of the three main exports from the city. According to a publication on the melon's history (yes, this fruit rates a booklet), compiled by Lee Taylor and Adrian Gould, a package of the fruit was sent overseas to King Edward VII; thereafter, melons shipped to hotels in Boston, Chicago, and New York were stamped with the royal name and commanded top dollar. Taylor and Gould characterize this time as a period of "Montreal melon madness," a mania fed by fashion and flavor.

The fruit's fortunes started to change in the 1920s, when melons that were easier to grow and transport began to dominate the market. The city's melon farms were plowed under for suburban

15

homes, and the Montreal Melon virtually disappeared in just a few decades. But not completely. In the mid-1990s Montreal writer Mark Abley tracked down a packet of seeds from an Iowa seed bank and passed some along to a local grower, Ken Taylor of Windmill Point Farm. The melon was suddenly back in cultivation and it has since caught on. Festivals have celebrated this unusually spicy musk melon; growers have held competitions to try to tip the scales with giants. And everyone who plants it is growing its story, cultivating its history.

STORIES ARE A very particular kind of knowledge—information multiplied and transformed through the creative and generative urge to share—but homegrown food also offers us a much more basic, and reassuring, form of knowledge. Quite simply, when we're the ones doing the planting and the growing, we know exactly where our food comes from. It is a rare commercial transaction where we can say this with much confidence. But for the food we produce ourselves, there's little doubt. In the language of agricultural production, we control the inputs.

To a degree, anyway. While we control what we add to the soil, we don't necessarily know what's already there. Many people who are thinking about growing food in cities raise this issue as a major concern. They worry that urban soils are, by definition, contaminated. It's prudent to wonder. But I'd argue that it's equally important to ask different questions as well. Do we know what's in the agricultural soils where the great majority of our food comes from—in China and Latin America, for example? Do we know what chemicals are regularly used to produce the fruits and vegetables grown globally and shipped to North America? Are any of these chemicals banned here but used elsewhere, and do any of these chemicals remain in the imported food we eat? According to the Progressive Policy Institute's 2007 report *Spoiled: Keeping Tainted Food Off America's Tables,* 98.7 percent of imported food is never inspected by the Food and Drug Administration (FDA) or the USDA. What are the health and environmental standards related to the use of sewage sludge on agricultural lands? Ask these questions and the soil in our cities might start to seem like something we can control, something a little less worrisome.

But definitely not altogether worry free. Each of us will find our own comfort level, but for anyone with even a smidgen of doubt about the health of their soil, there are some straightforward steps to take. In my first home, for example, I was worried about growing food beside the fence, which had the suspicious green glow of pressure-treated wood. (This was in the late 1980s, before chromated copper arsenate was a restricted-use product.) I certainly didn't want to eat any vegetables contaminated by the stuff. So I sent soil samples to the provincial environment ministry. The report came back that yes, there were elevated levels of heavy metals but still within consumption guidelines. I guess my comfort level has a slightly paranoid edge to it—I ditched the root vegetables and stuck with fruiting plants such as tomatoes, which absorb less in the way of metals from the soil. At my current home, however, in an area of Toronto that has no history of industrial activity, I didn't bother to do a soil test. Most of my vegetables are in pots, anyway. But at the community garden where I grow vegetables directly in the ground, we did have soil tests done. The site had formerly been a fire station, a lumber yard, and who knows what else. Again, the results weren't worrying, but we replaced the soil and built up the soil level in the beds just to be entirely safe.

Worrying about the health of our urban soils serves an obvious, useful purpose in that it often leads us to soil testing—a good

17

City Soil Safety

JUST HOW safe are urban soils for the growing of food? Short of having your soil tested, it's impossible to know for sure what contaminants might be present.

But there are risk factors you can take into account: exterior paints (on buildings and fences) that may have been applied before lead in paints was regulated; nearby industries or autobody shops that may be releasing or leaking toxic substances; historical industrial uses of your land; heavily traveled roads and highways in close proximity that may have left a legacy of elevated lead levels in soil from the era of leaded gasoline.

If any of these risk factors are present, it would be prudent to have your soil tested. In the U.S., contact the local agricultural extension agent or your city's public health or environment unit. In Canada, contact your province's environment ministry or your city's public health or environ- ment office. If a soil test reveals elevated lead levels, consider taking the following steps to reduce your risk:

> Use raised beds or containers filled with clean topsoil, and place a semi- permeable barrier, such as landscape cloth (available at nurseries or hardware stores), between the existing soil and the newly added soil.

> Maintain alkaline soil conditions (a pH of 7 or higher) through additions of lime, and add compost high in phosphate, which has been shown to reduce the mobility of lead in the soil, making it less likely to be absorbed by plants.

> Avoid inhaling dust or soil particles when gardening, and (it hardly needs saying) wear gloves and wash your hands after digging in the dirt.

> Wash all fruits and vegetables (some people recommend using deter- gent) before you eat them. This will remove the lead risk from any soil or dust adhering to the plant.

> If you're still worried, only grow fruiting crops, such as tomatoes, beans, peas, and squash, which absorb much less lead than root crops. (Leafy vegetables absorb more lead than fruiting crops but less than root crops.)

> Plant vegetables and fruits away from the foundations of buildings and painted surfaces.

> Finally, if you're an adventurous soul with time on your hands and a yen for home science experiments, a backyard phytoremediation project might be worth looking into. Phytoremediation involves the use of plants to accumulate contaminants and "clean" the soil; obviously, the plants are destroyed rather than eaten. Samantha Langley-Turnbaugh of the Department of Environmental Science and Policy at the University of Southern Maine did tests using spinach, sunflowers, and Indian mustard as phytoaccumulators for lead. She found that these plants, grown in soil with a pH of 5–6.5 (that is, moderately acidic) and with low organic matter, removed at least 100 ppm of lead from the soil after one growing season. Interestingly, a community garden in Portland, on land owned by the Oregon Sustainable Agriculture Land Trust (OSALT), is in the early stages of experimenting with a low-tech, low-cost method of remediating lead-contaminated soil. Using plants to take up lead, then composting the plants and spreading the compost throughout the site, the researchers are studying whether it is possible to disperse the existing lead evenly and lower the readings to safe levels on the whole site. "The traditional way to deal with lead contamination is to dig it up and put it somewhere else. That's not sustainable—it just makes it someone else's problem," explains Will Newman II of OSALT. "We're experimenting with spreading it evenly into a larger area, to see if we can reduce the total lead burden on site to a low enough level to grow food."

first step if we plan to eat what comes out of the ground. But it's valuable in another way, too. That worry encourages us to pose questions and delve into the state of our urban environment. And I suspect that the more we learn, the more surprised, and possibly outraged, we'll be. Who is dumping what where, with legal sanction? Do our laws require disclosure? Is that information available to the public? Do we really know, or is there any meaningful way to find out, what surrounds us in the air, lurks in the ground, swirls in our water? How would our cities change if we all started asking these questions? For the better, no doubt.

I know, I know, we just want to grow some good tomatoes, not necessarily change the world! But that's the wonderfully insidious thing about food gardening. It creeps in and takes us places we didn't expect to go. Consider garbage, for instance. You will know that you are garden-obsessed when you begin to scout your neighborhood on garbage day looking for bags of dead leaves. (You can never have too many leaves for mulching purposes, leaves for leaf-mold production, leaves for compost-making.) From there, it's not too much of a conceptual leap to wonder: why is my city wasting this precious resource, sending leaves to the dump? Or, for those of us lucky enough to live in a city that already composts organic waste, to ask the questions: is the compost my city produces of high-enough quality to use on my food garden, and if not, why not, and does the city make this compost readily available to any gardener who wants some?

In sometimes subtle, sometimes declarative ways, the food garden takes us to politics. We may not acknowledge it as such (*I am just growing tomatoes!*), and there's no imperative in the equation that says we must consider it in such terms, but politics hovers around the edges of urban food production.

And sometimes front and center. Ten years ago, one rarely heard the term "food miles." Now, the large U.K. supermarket

20

chain Tesco labels some of its products with carbon footprint figures, showing how many grams of carbon were emitted as a result
of growing, manufacturing, transporting, and storing the product.
In a relatively short time, we have begun to add greenhouse gas
emissions to the mental ledger on which we do the accounting for
our decisions. The focus of our guilt seems to shift regularly. One
year it's SUVs people apologize for (if they own one) or deplore (if
they don't). Another year it's airplane travel in the shame spotlight, relegated to the status of carbon indulgence the planet can
no longer afford.

While a guilty conscience is a great motivator, and awareness
of the impact of our choices is always good, I wonder if we're not
in danger of missing the bigger picture when we focus exclusively
on the personal. By all means consider whether or not each and
every car trip is necessary, but walking or biking or taking the
bus to the store won't change the fact that the items for sale at
that store got there through a system based on globalization, cen-
tralization, and concentration. As writer and food-policy expert
Wayne Roberts has pointed out, so much of the current focus
on "buy local" downloads the responsibility (and the guilt) to the
consumer, yet the system itself—a system of government and corporate policies—does little to support, and meaningfully supply,
consumer desire for the local.

Nowhere are the carbon costs of such a system more clus-
tered and readily locatable than at the food store. According to the
United Nations Food and Agriculture Organization (FAO), agriculture, along with deforestation and land-use changes related to
agriculture, generates, globally, one-third of the total man-made
emissions of greenhouse gases, including one-half of methane
emissions and three-quarters of nitrous oxide emissions. That's
a lot of belching cows and a lot of nitrogen fertilizers. Indeed,
the UN calculates that animal farming alone accounts for more

21

greenhouse gas emissions (almost one-fifth) than all the cars, trucks, and planes in the world combined.

Well, we gotta eat. But we don't need to eat a globalized, centralized, and corporately concentrated menu. And if we didn't, the food-miles portion of the greenhouse-gas-emissions pie, as it relates to agriculture, would be a significantly smaller slice. There are researchers who spend their days calculating such things (Just as there are researchers who spend their days complicating the calculations with "what if's," "but's," and "have you thought of that's"). Given that the distance food travels has been steadily increasing for the past fifty years, what they've found is hardly surprising, but what they've now calculated is how that distance translates into atmospheric emissions.

Marc Xuereb, a public health planner with the Region of Waterloo Public Health department in Ontario, conducted a study, published in 2005, that looked at fifty-eight commonly eaten imported foods, all of which could be grown or raised in Waterloo Region. The study found that the imported items traveled almost 4,500 kilometers on average to reach the dinner tables of that southern Ontario city, producing through transit 51,709 tonnes of greenhouse gas emissions annually (5.9 percent of the greenhouse gas emissions generated by households in the region). The report notes that this is equivalent to more than a quarter tonne per household, or more than 16,000 cars on the road. The study also calculated how the emissions would compare if the imported items were instead sourced locally or regionally, from within a 30-kilometer radius. Under that scenario, greenhouse gas emissions were reduced by almost 99 percent—from 51,709 tonnes for the imported items to 2,224 tonnes for the local items, a savings of 49,485 tonnes. (Even within a distance of 250 kilometers, the local items represented savings, in greenhouse gas emissions, of 96 percent.)

Other studies bring these numbers down to dinner-plate level. The Toronto nonprofit organization FoodShare, for example, went on two shopping trips in 2003 for the ingredients of a typical meal (lamb chops, sweet potatoes, Swiss chard, carrots, salad, and fruit): one trip to a farmers' market and the other to a supermarket. Using the product labels to compare the origins of the food, they found that the supermarket items traveled, on average, eighty-one times farther than the farmers' market items. They calculated that a year of choosing local over imported foods would save a half-tonne of greenhouse gas emissions per household.

Of course, such comparisons carry all the practical deficiencies of any ecological footprint analysis. Things are just too complicated for any straightforward calculation to take all the variables into account. And how far back in the complex chain of production can researchers—should researchers—go anyway? While it's clear that in terms of simple tailpipe emissions trucking trumps air freight, how much would that calculation change—and how much more complicated would it become—if it included the emissions resulting from highway construction? Likewise, how does one account for the infinite variations in growing methods used across the globe? A totally non-mechanized farm in India certainly uses less energy to grow its crops than most farms in North America. So even if the food arrived here in the biggest fuel-guzzling jumbo jet there is, it could still have a lower energy footprint than its North American equivalent. As a 1997 Swedish study found, it might indeed be more energy efficient for eaters in that northern country to buy Spanish-grown tomatoes rather than local greenhouse tomatoes because Spain's climate is conducive to heat-loving crops, whereas Swedish production requires great gobs of energy to keep greenhouse tomatoes growing.

Even principles that we might think provide certainty and comfort in this morass of complication—for example, thinking

23

local is always more energy efficient than regional—are not straightforward. A 2001 study done by the Leopold Center for Sustainable Agriculture at Iowa State University found that a local food system can require more energy and emit more carbon dioxide than its regional counterpart when the trucks used to supply local foods are smaller than the trucks delivering regionally produced food. The smaller trucks require more trips, thus negating the carbon savings of food grown closer to market. In other words, longer distances don't always equal higher emissions.

Another criticism leveled against food-miles analyses is that they're too focused on one simple measure—energy—and ignore a whole host of other factors. Any complete accounting of the impact of our food choices would need to consider water use, biodiversity values, animal welfare, labor practices, income distribution, and soil erosion, to name the most obvious examples. And, of course, hovering around the edges of the food-miles discussion are the broader, and arguably much more important, issues of security, sovereignty, autonomy, and control. If we depend on food from around the globe to feed us, can we really consider ourselves to be safe, secure, and sovereign? As Mark Bittman points out in his book *Food Matters,* "America no longer grows enough edible fruits and vegetables for everyone to eat our own government's recommended five servings a day." In other words, we are vulnerable and dependent on factors over which we have little or no control.

It's enough to make one despair at the impossibility of ever making meaningful, sustainable decisions about what we eat from where. Is there no simple principle that can guide us? I'd suggest that there is one, right in front of us. As we stand in the food aisles, confused by the choices, trying to make good ones, we can ask ourselves a question that goes much deeper than distance and is much more revealing: is it possible to truly locate the source of a particular food and meaningfully determine the details

24

of its production? When we shift our focus from proximity to traceability, it doesn't necessarily mean that we need to do the all-consuming work of tracing the sources and conditions. (Who has the time for shopping excursions as investigative reporting projects?) No, what it means is that we determine whether or not it's actually *possible* to trace the source, should we choose to exercise such informed control over what we consume.

If this seems like one too many questions at the supermarket, Canadian writer Noah Richler has proposed another, admittedly much more pleasure-ful, principle to guide us, one that I think we could all happily follow. In an essay about local food, published in 2008 in the *Toronto Star*, he offers this grace note: "the better arbiter is the palate's common sense." Amen to that. In the final analysis, we don't necessarily need to agonize over the complexity of it all. We don't need to pore over the data of competing studies, wondering if the use of the Weighted Average Source Distance formula rather than the Weighted Average Emissions Ratio formula is really a methodological research flaw. Because in the end, it comes down to fresh flavor, the palate's commonsense judgement of what tastes best: the strawberry near or the strawberry far? And that is a question all of us can answer for ourselves.

OKAY, I HEAR what you're thinking. In fact, I share the thought. It's easy enough to talk about the benefits, to compare home-grown strawberries to imported strawberries and know which one will win the taste test. But there's something missing and, for me, what's missing can best be summed up with two words, two words that strike a dagger into the heart of my "let's grow as much of our own food as we can" enthusiasm: coffee and chocolate.

When I went to see a presentation by Alisa Smith and J.B. MacKinnon, the engaging writers behind the book *The 100-Mile Diet,* I felt inspired by their talk, energized by their passion, and

25

awed by their gumption. But I sat there the whole hour with the words coffee and chocolate on the tip of my tongue—and not just because it was a lunch-hour presentation and my stomach was grumbling.

You might have different words in mind—pineapples, cinnamon, and cashews, perhaps—but the point remains. We crave access to foods that we just can't grow in North America's climate. Not only do we crave them, but we expect that they will be available pretty much everywhere, all the time. Our choices and desires march to the imperative of *now*.

Allow me a digression that you've probably heard before—probably from a grandparent. And yes, it starts with the phrase *when I was growing up*. Back then, if there was a movie you wanted to see, there was a two-week window of opportunity at the local cinema, and then it was gone. If you were lucky, it would reappear on television (on one of the four channels) in about a year, but if you happened to be out or your TV's reception was wonky that night, you missed it again. No videotaping, no downloading, no pirate DVDs in the dollar stores. Or let's say you found yourself low on cash—at nine PM on a Saturday night. Disaster. The banks were only open during the week, and only for very limited hours during the day. No bank machines or debit cards, and few places took credit.

In short, life—its pleasures and necessities—required planning for the future, taking the future into account in our decisions and perhaps, if necessary, delaying gratification.

And here I will get more grandparent-ish by saying: is advance planning and occasional delayed gratification such a bad thing? Isn't it, in fact, one of the grand cognitive features that distinguishes adults from children, humans from other animals? Okay, strike that. I'm sure foxes spend a lot of time planning their next

26

hunt, and kids are masters of scheming ahead for the next treat. But as an adult, human pursuit, I'd say that advance planning defines a great deal of what's best in us. Just as a lack of advance planning defines the worst. If we were to pick the most dire of global problems, wouldn't we agree that a common culprit in all of them is an entirely id-directed focus on the now at the expense of what's to come?

If that sounds like shrill moralizing, let's cut the id some slack. Because the id—guided as it is by the pleasure principle—suffers in all this, too. Another *when I was growing up* example, this one food-related and, I'm afraid, rather clichéd. But truly, we really did get a mandarin orange in our Christmas stocking, stuffed at the bottom of the toe end. To me, it tasted better than any candy, and it was a treat I looked forward to all year. It was from a faraway place and we valued it as something special. Now, I'm never without at least one box of mandarin oranges from October to February. I eat them like cheap candy. And, alas, the experience of them has indeed been cheapened for me. I still put the label from the season's first box on the fridge (it *is* a banner occasion in my life's calendar), but something's been lost. I eat them and love them, but by the third or fourth box, they aren't quite as special. They enter the autumn routine, and at least some of their sharply satisfying flavor gets sanded down through repetition.

One of the defining features of our time is the slow and steady erosion of seasonality. As the specificities of seasonal changes get lost, we progress into sameness. And it's in the sphere of food that the loss of seasonality can be felt most acutely. One by one, the foods that once marked a particular period of time—a window of taste—have devolved into a condition of always available. I first noticed it with peas, then cherries and raspberries. I thought asparagus and peaches were holdouts, until about a decade ago,

27

> The Benefits of Growing Your Own Food in the City

- > It saves you money.
- > You'll enjoy some of the freshest and most nutritious food you'll ever eat, as fewer nutrients are lost in storage and transportation.
- > It involves zero packaging.
- > You'll know where your food comes from and what's required to grow it.
- > The activity of gardening gets you outside and stretching.
- > Nothing's more local than the 10-foot diet—and it's great for assuaging carbon footprint guilt.
- > Every homegrown bite takes you out of a broken, profit-driven food system that feeds us fat, salt, and sugar.
- > You can grow varieties of fruits and vegetables that aren't available commercially.
- > Chances are you'll eat more vegetables.
- > By recycling organic waste, you'll be turning a waste product into a resource: compost.

- > Food gardening is a creative recreation that will give you immensely satisfying results.
- > Food crops increase urban biodiversity and habitat for pollinators and enhance the soil.
- > Fruit and vegetable gardens can be creatively designed to add beauty—and surprise—to the ornamental landscape.
- > Food gardening calms the mind and enriches the soul and belly.
- > Tinkering in the garden provides an outlet for exercising the caring gene.
- > By growing food, you're participating in an ancient skill that too many of us have lost.
- > Gardening weaves food in a meaningful, productive way into our everyday lives.

when South American imports started to appear in my local stores in the winter. About the only truly seasonal fruits and vegetables left—in my city anyway—are corn on the cob and watermelon. Their window of availability remains intact.

I'm sure that to some ears, this sounds like the strangest of whining complaints. Why on earth would we be anything but thrilled by the fact that we can eat raspberries in January? Our options have expanded. Our desires are sated. Our taste buds are tickled. But I wonder if we haven't lost celebration.

Of all our basic needs—to breathe, to sleep, to eat—food is the one most strongly associated with celebration. Special occasions call for special meals. These unique but repeated events punctuate the progression of our lives. As, at one time in our not too distant past, did the march of seasonal fruits and vegetables through the calendar. Even if the appearance of the first juicy pear of the year wasn't accompanied by some kind of ceremony to mark the occasion, surely our taste buds did a little jig. But it's much harder to carve out moments of conscious celebration when we've been lulled (and, I'd argue, dulled) by constant availability. Ho hum, it's just another pear, like the one I had last month, and the month before that, and the month before that, every month in fact.

Growing some of our own food, on the other hand, links us with seasonal celebration and conscious consumption. The fact that we can't pick peas from our backyards in August heightens our appreciation for the pea-picking possibilities of early summer. The seasons of the garden give and they withhold—and celebration marks their passage.

As for the coffee and chocolate (and pineapples, cinnamon, and cashews), no way am I giving them up. (And I'd snarl at anyone who tried to guilt me into it.) But let's eat them while alert to the choices, priorities, and values that deliver them to our plates, aware of the privilege and the cost that make the impossible-to-grow-here, possible-to-eat-here. And while we're at it, when we're fired up on coffee and chocolate, let's devote some of that caffeine- and sugar-fueled energy to creating alternative structures that support local foods and local farmers, and thus make the grown-here as economically viable (for farmers and eaters) as the grown-elsewhere.

IT'S EASY ENOUGH for the well fed to wax on about celebration, feel virtuous about reduced food miles, and feel nostalgic about seasonal pleasures, but when a food garden is occasioned by necessity, the food grown takes on a different sheen. It can mean a meal that includes fresh and healthy vegetables when all that's available at the food bank are packaged items. It can mean good nutrition when food dollars otherwise couldn't be stretched beyond inexpensive processed foods. It can mean easier access to readily available produce when the closest supermarket is miles away in a tonier section of town. It can mean food bounty in a food desert.

However much our culture tells us that widespread food production doesn't belong in cities; however much we may fear the challenges unique to urban food-growing efforts; however much our gardening desires may be tempered by limitations of time and space; however comfortable we've become in the role of global consumers rather than local producers—in short, whatever the personal, social, and political obstacles in the way of a more committed embrace of urban food-growing potential, maybe all we really need to do is to open ourselves up to possibility. If we look around and ask ourselves about all the *could's* that surround us, chances are very good indeed that we will find places of possibility, ideas of do-ability, and corners ripe for sowing and reaping.

30

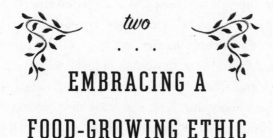

two

. . .

EMBRACING A

FOOD-GROWING ETHIC

ON THE FIRST day of spring, in 2009, a busy mom took time out of her highly scheduled work day to do something unusual. She dug up a patch of lawn and prepared the soil for a vegetable garden in the front yard. Spinach, chard, collard greens, and black kale seedlings would go into the ground where only grass had flourished. A small space of edibility was thus carved out of an ornamental landscape. And not just any ornamental landscape: this was the front yard of a nation, the White House lawn in Washington, D.C., and the mom holding the hoe was Michelle Obama.

Was it something in the water? Or maybe in the air? In the spring and summer of 2009, politicians of all stripes and at every level, in the U.S. and Canada, were planting food gardens at the symbolic seats of power—in front of city halls, governors' mansions, legislatures, and yes, even on the lawn of the White House.

Michelle Obama had plenty of help. The National Park Service had tested the soil (and found lead levels of 93 parts per million, within the safe range) and prepared the bed. Twenty-six grade 5 schoolchildren from the nearby Bancroft Elementary School assisted with the planting. An army of media recorded every move and dissected every nuance, right down to the First Lady's choice of footwear: Jimmy Choo boots. While the folksiness of the scene may have been diminished somewhat by the luxury attire adorning her feet, the popular verdict on the event was that this was a class act by a down-to-earth woman in touch with the people. In a few brief hours, Obama achieved what food activists and nutrition advocates could only dream of: she made the planting of a vegetable garden front page news around the world. It was a good news day indeed for urban agriculture.

As is appropriate for a place on which the spotlight of symbolism shines so brightly, the White House front yard has been the focus of many food-related campaigns over the years, some started by individuals or groups with a message to promote, others initiated by the inhabitants of 1600 Pennsylvania Avenue themselves. Surely the spirit of Eleanor Roosevelt was hovering over the White House lawn to cheer Obama on. It was Roosevelt who last channeled her energies in the direction of food production, planting a Victory Garden at the White House during World War II. Interestingly, Roosevelt's efforts, while embraced by the people, were somewhat less than enthusiastically supported by officials at the U.S. Department of Agriculture, who were concerned about the effects that a populace committed to growing their own food in backyards across the nation would have on the agricultural sector and the food industry. How times have changed. When Obama planted her garden, U.S. Secretary of Agriculture Tom Vilsack had just recently announced that an organic food garden, "The People's Garden," would be planted at USDA headquarters, across from the Smithsonian Mall, in honor of President Lincoln. For the photo op accompanying the announcement, Vilsack chipped away at the pavement—a reversal of fortune for the parking lot, which was brought back to some semblance of paradise. As he put it to the assembled media: "Our goal is for USDA facilities worldwide to install community gardens in their local offices."

Other presidential precedents can be found for Obama's agricultural act. The first presidential inhabitant of the White House, John Adams, planted vegetables there. Thomas Jefferson planted fruit trees. President William Taft is said to have kept a cow at the White House from 1910 to 1913—a Holstein-Friesian gifted by a senator from Wisconsin. During Woodrow Wilson's tenure, sheep grazed the lawn. In the late 1970s, Jimmy Carter tended an herb garden.

The symbolic power carried by food production at this most symbolic of households had been noted and promoted by many people and organizations before Obama picked up her trowel. In a slyly subversive gesture, Euell Gibbons, the father of modern food foraging whose classic 1962 book, *Stalking the Wild Asparagus,* is still in print, stuck his hand through the White House fence and plucked four edible "weeds" from the lawn. Clearly the standards of care have become more stringent since then, and the small army of groundskeepers who maintain the place wouldn't let any weeds—edible or not—get past them.

It was precisely this small army that writer Michael Pollan, the author of many bestselling books, including *The Omnivore's Dilemma,* suggested in 1991 be enlisted for a different kind of effort. His *New York Times* opinion piece "Abolish the White House Lawn" proposed that President Bush issue an executive order to rip out the grass—"an act of environmental shock therapy" that, Pollan imagined, "could conceivably set off a revolution in consciousness." Just where that revolution could lead included

33

four different possible destinations, usefully provided by Pollan. One option was to replace the lawn with a meadow, the mown path of which could form a spur of the Appalachian Trail. Another was to restore a portion of the White House landscape to its original condition—as wetland. (Pollan acknowledged that the swamp symbolism might be troubling to some.) A third proposal was to plant a vegetable garden—an 18-acre Victory Garden. "The White House has enough land to become self-sufficient in food—a model of Jeffersonian independence and thrift!" Pollan noted. The fourth suggestion, preferred by Pollan, was to plant an orchard with that most American of fruits, the apple. (Pollan remained silent on the subject of apple pie.)

President Bush didn't accept Pollan's challenge, and it took almost two decades for the White House turfgrass to be turfed—1,100 square feet of it anyway. We can only speculate about what role Roger Doiron played in the Obamas' decision to install a White House food garden, but there's no doubt that his persuasive efforts captured the public's imagination. Doiron is the person behind the Maine-based network Kitchen Gardeners International's Eat the View campaign. Promoting "high-impact food gardens in high-profile places," his campaign was launched in February 2008 to encourage the planting of a White House Victory Garden (for the "Eaters in Chief"). More than 110,000 people signed the petition. Without a doubt, the garden has been an inspiration to hundreds of thousands more—an example of a leader pointing people in the direction of positive, personal solutions in tough times. But it's also a rousing example of the people leading the chief.

Cynics might suggest that the White House garden is all optics without much traction, despite the flurry of interest that accompanied its planting. But the follow-through has been impressive.

Michelle Obama, who said at the September 2009 opening of a Washington, D.C., farmers' market that the White House food garden was "one of the greatest things I've done in my life so far," has put food issues in the spotlight. According to the website Obama Foodorama, which tracks matters food-related, Michelle Obama is "the only First Lady to ever have a food policy agenda, a food policy team, and a Food Initiative Coordinator." Indeed, she has been a food garden ambassador of sorts well beyond Washington. When the Obamas went to the U.K. in April 2009, the First Lady encouraged Prime Minister Gordon Brown's wife to plant a food garden at Number 10 Downing Street. And on her second international trip, to Russia, Obama was greeted by a Moscow media obsessed with her gardening activity—a refreshing change, a substantive change, from the focus on her fashion sense. Gardens as an instrument of international diplomacy . . . now that's an idea with growing power.

Closer to home, all across North America, what might be called politically symbolic food gardens are sprouting up at a great rate in landscapes of power and governance. In the spring of 2009 alone, Maria Shriver, wife of California governor Arnold Schwarzenegger, announced plans to plant a vegetable garden at Capitol Park in Sacramento; Maryland's First Lady, Judge Katie O'Malley, planted a food garden at the governor's mansion in Annapolis; Portland mayor Sam Adams inaugurated one at his city hall, replacing two small lawns with vegetables, while the Portland headquarters of Multnomah County installed the Hope Garden; Baltimore mayor Shiela Dixon proclaimed that a food garden would be planted on the plaza outside city hall, and Vancouver mayor Gregor Robertson converted a portion of the city hall lawn into a community garden that includes wheelchair-accessible plots. The governors of Maine, Pennsylvania, and New York all have food gardens at their official residences, according to Eat the View's Roger Doiron.

It's a brave politician indeed who risks the jokes and humorous digs that such gardening activity might provoke. As one wag on the Society of Environmental Journalists listserv, Mark Neuzil, put it, "Allow me to be the first to say that these [politicians] will have no shortage of manure with which to fertilize their vegetables." And it's a brave activist who takes food matters into his or her own hands by planting symbolic food gardens in public, political places. Matthew Behrens was arrested for the garden he and other members of the group Toronto Action for Social Change planted at Queen's Park, on the grounds of the Ontario Legislature, in the mid-1990s. About forty people showed up with bags of topsoil, seed packets, and small transplants in front of the imposing Romanesque building and proceeded to plant zucchinis, peas, and tomatoes under the premier's window. They also put in some marigolds, not as a concession to aesthetics but for pest control. As a seventy-five-year-old nun watered seedlings, security guards swooped in, demanding to know how long the gardeners intended to be there. Presumably the guards were not amused when one of the protesters looked at the back of the zucchini seed pack and said, "fifty-two days." Behrens and a few others were arrested, fingerprinted, and held overnight in jail—all for adding topsoil to the heavily compacted ground and sprinkling some seeds.

The group returned to Queen's Park the following autumn to plant winter wheat and Jerusalem artichokes. Ten people were arrested, but acquitted at trial. There was no evidence that they'd damaged public property; indeed, common sense and the evidence both suggested that the gardeners had instead improved the health of the soil. Unsuccessful in official attempts to punish this wanton act of *gardening*, one exasperated police sergeant was quoted in *NOW*, Toronto's alternative magazine, as saying: "It's not like we're upset that they're planting seeds, but there's got to be a line. Otherwise, everyone and their uncle would be there growing things."

Now that's a scary thought. And also a thought blind to historical precedence. Everyone and their uncle *did* in fact grow things—lots of things in lots of places, including on the legislature grounds—during at least three notable periods in North American history: during World War I, the Depression, and World War II. Variously labeled as war gardens, relief gardens, and Victory Gardens, these massive efforts at domestic, home-based food production were hugely successful by any measure. Fruit and vegetable gardens sprang up everywhere there was space: in backyards and front yards, parks, utility corridors, vacant lots, school grounds, church grounds, playing fields, community centers, corporate grounds, railway corridors... Name a type of private or public space and it was planted. Likewise, the commitment to food production cut across all social classes, from the poorest to the richest, from the powerful to the disenfranchised. Picture this: millionaire socialite Helena Rubinstein had a penthouse Victory Garden (she called it her "Farm in the Sky") at her Park Avenue apartment in New York City. Along with growing cauliflower, cabbage, and celery, she kept two chickens and two rabbits. At a 1943 Victory Garden party she hosted in honor of the United States Crop Corps, an organization of auxiliary farm workers recruited by the War Manpower Commission to grow food, surrealist painter Salvador Dali mingled with the assembled crowd.

The North American public enthusiastically embraced domestic food production during both world wars, proving that a staggering amount of food could be grown, particularly in cities, if people set their minds to it. During World War I, an estimated 5 million gardeners in America produced $520 million worth of food in 1918, cultivated in backyards, vacant lots, and previously

37

untilled land; the National War Garden Commission in the U.S. (just the fact that such a commission existed speaks volumes) called them "patriotic gifts . . . to the nation."

What is perhaps most striking—particularly for today's audience—is the earnest urgency of the government's language around the need for domestic food production. During WWI, the Ontario Department of Agriculture steeped its garden promotion in military metaphors intended to galvanize the populace. "Have You Enlisted in The Greater Production Battalion?" asked a full-page advertisement the department published in the April 1918 edition of *The Canadian Horticulturist*. Likewise, a department circular, titled "A Vegetable Garden for Every Home," stated that "every backyard is fighting ground for the empire." Noting that the government planned to ban the sale of canned goods (in order to preserve supplies for the war effort), the department warned that "if we don't grow them [vegetables], we won't have them." Rarely does a government entity summarize a situation with such bracing clarity.

Nor did the end of the hostilities in Europe bring an end to North American food production campaigns. In 1919, the National War Garden Commission stated, "As a result of emergency created by war the home garden of America has become an institution of world-wide importance." Characterizing home food gardens as that "which helped establish the balance of power between starvation and abundance," the commission urged Americans to engage in "high pressure food production."

North Americans responded to the call again during World War II. According to the U.S. Department of Agriculture, 20 million Victory Gardens produced 40 percent of America's fresh vegetables in 1943. In Canada, according to the federal Department of Agriculture, 115 million pounds of vegetables were grown in 209,200 urban gardens in that same year. There were, of course, thousands more wartime gardens in villages and on farms.

Such commitment to the food-growing effort didn't just spontaneously spring forth from the collective consciousness of the North American urban populace. It arose in response to policies and promotional campaigns that worked to organize public purpose. At all levels of government, in both the U.S. and Canada, officials drove home the message—often couched in patriotic terms—that gardens were a matter of "duty."

For example, the federal government appealed to Canadians during WWII with the following bold and baldly stated goal: "Every available bit of land that is suitable should be put into a garden. Those with experience should help their neighbours who wish to start." The feds advised provincial governments that it was "desirable to sponsor community garden and backyard garden campaigns." Cities across Canada took up the charge. Victoria, British Columbia, offered concessions to the public at $5 a year to grow gardens on vacant lots. Toronto, Ontario, offered the use of municipally owned lots to individuals and groups for gardening purposes, charging just 25 cents for a permit; interestingly, the fee covered police protection for the gardens. Even Toronto's mayor got in the act, arranging a photo op with the *Globe and Mail,* which dutifully reported that Mayor Fred Conboy's flower border was replaced with tomatoes and that his lawn was being transformed into a potato patch.

Citizens responded with all-out effort. The police and firemen at the Forest Hill Village station in Toronto cut four patches out of their 5,000-square-foot lawn. As the *Globe* described it in June 1943, they used "any odd time they [could] spare from upholding the law and keeping firefighting equipment in tip-top condition" to grow tomatoes, radishes, Scotch kale, carrots, cabbages, and more.

The Ontario Hydro Horticultural Club's Victory Garden Committee had 425 members in Toronto alone (750 throughout the province) gardening on land donated by municipal commissions and private owners. In Toronto, they grew $26,000 (or $331,000 in 2009 dollars) worth of food in 1943. The Community Gardens Association of Toronto tended plots on major streets, cultivating $30,940 worth of vegetables. The Pine Crescent Joy Club, an east-end Toronto activity club for youngsters, turned the lawn, where once they enjoyed badminton, horseshoes, and lawn bowling, into a 35-foot-long, V-shaped Victory Garden. Seed companies did a roaring business: in response to a reporter's inquiries, one seed seller responded, "We're so busy selling seeds for Victory gardens that we have no time to even discuss them."

All this food-focused labor bore results across the country. By the end of the 1943 growing season, there were approximately 52,000 Victory Gardens in the greater Vancouver area, which together produced 31,000 tons of fruits and vegetables valued at $4 million. Many Vancouverites also applied to the City Building and Zoning Secretary for permission to keep more than twelve chickens (permits weren't required for fewer than twelve), though this pales in comparison to the livestock action in Britain, where, according to Michael Hough's book *Cities and Natural Process* (first published in 1984 as *City Form and Natural Process*), keeping chickens, pigs, goats and bees "evolved as a major urban activity" during the war: "By 1943 there were 4,000 pig clubs comprising some 110,000 members keeping 105,000 pigs."

The British effort no doubt provided inspiration for many North American Victory Garden campaigns. Images of British citizens growing food in craters left by bombs and using the Tower of London moat to grow cabbages were surely potent motivation for North Americans to assist in the war effort by growing food

anywhere and everywhere. Even the royal family was tending vegetable gardens at Buckingham Palace and Windsor Castle.

Although it might seem inappropriate to make the connection,
there are striking parallels between then and now. Global conflict
threatened and continues to threaten our ability to take care of our
most basic needs. For us in North America, the threat may not be
as immediate, but it hovers in the background because our society
is now far more global. We are more connected to, and dependent
upon, other parts of the world than ever before. Today, as a result
of many factors, including the recession, close to 4 million Americans and 3.4 million Canadians live in poverty and struggle to
feed themselves adequately, relying on food banks, food stamps,
and charitable organizations to supplement their diet. Although
the particular circumstances of past world wars, the Depression,
and the current climate are vastly different, there remains a common thread: millions of North Americans are in need, and one of
the basic things they need is food. In this context, are the times
not ripe to nurture the resilience—resilience that sprang, literally,
from the soil—that helped North Americans through not-too-
distant times of conflict and economic hardship?

Perhaps the "yes we can" that we need to proclaim—beyond
symbolic gesture, and from the soil—is the yes we can of feeding
ourselves. And it would be useful to remember, while we flex our
yes we can muscles, that not too long ago, yes we did.

JUST WHEN AND why did we lose that commitment to domestic food production? And, equally important, how? What were
the mechanisms at work to help create a cultural amnesia around
our ability to feed ourselves? Was it a collective decision to so
emphatically negate the food-producing possibilities of the city?
Or was it rather a slow accretion of factors, each building upon the

other, until we had forgotten the productive potential of our urban environments?

I suspect that we were willing participants in the erasure of food growing from our cities, at first anyway. World War II was over, and with it went need, replaced with want. There were products to buy and there was work to do in order to be prosperous enough to purchase all those consumer goods. Our homes became places of display, the stage on which the trappings of accumulated wealth could signal success. A profusion of food plants had no place in that display; they spoke of need, not ordered control. Much better to carpet our home landscapes with lawn—the ultimate symbol of triumph over necessity, a declarative public statement that we no longer depended on our yards to have the capacity to supply food, since the stores (and later the supermarkets) did that just fine. We had reached a heightened position of luxury in which space could be "wasted" and sustenance replaced with decoration; ornament was what we wanted. (I'll be talking about this in more detail in chapter 5.)

There were—and still are—class elements to this attitude. The suggestion of need that accompanies food gardens was, for a long time, something to hide rather than trumpet. To be forced by economic necessity to grow some of your own food was a public announcement of straitened circumstance and reduced status. For a brief period in the 1970s, the back-to-the-land movement— ironically, a movement characterized by privilege—attempted to invert the equation, rebranding need as a moral virtue, food growing as an ethical requirement. It's easy to imagine that those who didn't have the financial option of "dropping out" were less than entranced by the message.

As a teenager, I saw a similar thing happen, not only as it relates to class and food gardening, but to issues around ethnicity. At my high school, most of the students' fathers (and it was

42

> Converting a Lawn to a Vegetable Bed

A NO-DIG TECHNIQUE called sheet mulching is the easiest way to convert an area of lawn into a vegetable garden bed. Start preparing the bed in fall and you'll have wonderful soil ready to plant in the spring.

> Mow the existing grass using the lowest setting on your lawn mower. No need to rake up the clippings; just leave them where they land.

> Cover the area with a layer of cardboard or newspapers (if using newspapers, add a layer approximately ten sheets thick; if using cardboard, a single layer is fine, though be sure to remove any staples and packing tape).

> Spread a 3-inch layer of soil and/or soil mixed with compost and/or well-rotted manure on top of the cardboard or newspapers.

> Top it all off with a 3-inch layer of chopped dead leaves.

> Don't worry if, in spring, all of the cardboard and/or newspapers haven't completely decomposed; just dig planting holes through any cardboard or newspaper that remains.

the early to mid '70s, so it was mainly the dads) worked in blue collar jobs at the local automotive assembly plant, and most were recent immigrants from southern Italy. Food gardens were the norm in the culture of my large town—our neighborhood, anyway. (We had, by this point, moved from the small city where I'd spent my early years, where food gardens were rare.) Grape arbors covered the driveways, tomato plants flourished in backyards, and in autumn the air was redolent with the heady smells of wine and sauce production. My classmates, the children of immigrants, wanted nothing to do with it. For the most part, they looked on their parents' food-growing and food-preserving labor with embarrassment. They viewed their parents as hopelessly attached to old-country ways and they couldn't wait to leave such nostalgia—and nostalgia's food gardens—behind.

Our historical complicity in the triumphant rush to create landscapes of ornament rather than those satisfying need was also accompanied by economic and structural changes that have severely diminished our capacity to feed ourselves. In the past fifty years, we have created a food system that depends on global circulation and that is vulnerable to everything from minor hiccups to major disruptions in the global market. We're so inured to this long-distance choreography of goods that we fail to see its surreal logic. (Economist Herman Daly, in a 1993 *Scientific American* article, says it best: "Americans import Danish sugar cookies, and Danes import American sugar cookies. Exchanging recipes would surely be more efficient.") In my own city of Toronto, for example, as Debbie Field, the executive director of the nonprofit organization FoodShare, pointed out in *NOW* magazine in 2009, "There is more arable land in downtown Toronto than there is in Newfoundland." And yet, of the food consumed in Toronto, approximately 50 to 60 percent is imported, mostly from Florida, California, and Mexico.

Moving from the local to the regional level, the province of Ontario imports $4 billion more in food than it exports—this in a province that boasts more than 50 percent of Canada's Class 1 farmland. The great majority of our country's agricultural land is not devoted to what can be directly consumed—instead, just 6 percent of Canada's farms produce fruits and vegetables. Nor would it necessarily take a massive shift to rectify the imbalance and thus be able to meet our own needs rather than depending on global production. A Region of Waterloo Public Health study, for example, found that with a shift in production on just 10 to 12 percent of local agricultural lands in that region—replacing the foods we eat too much of (such as meat and highly processed foods) with the whole grains, legumes, fruits, and vegetables we don't eat enough of from local lands—the regional population could sustain itself from local agricultural lands. (The study assumed that people would continue to eat imports of many foods, such as bananas, that don't grow in the region.)

Retooling the food system in favor of the local and the regional, regaining control of what we eat and where it comes from, will require structural changes to every link in the long and complex chain that takes our food from seed to mouth. But reimagining our cities as places of committed food production, as one piece in that larger project, will require, above all else, not a shift in structure but a shift in attitude. Quite simply, the biggest barrier is an idea, a pervasive notion that food production does not *belong* in the city. Whether we came to this idea through a class-based discomfort that equates food growing with reduced economic status, or through other cultural channels (as my high school classmates did, viewing food growing as an ethnic marker of "otherness"), makes little difference, because the idea is now thoroughly entrenched, whatever its origins.

But there is a chink in the armor that surrounds our notion of what's proper, what's appropriate, what kinds of activities belong in the city. And that chink, that opening, lies in how we define the idea of urban productivity. What if we expanded our current yardsticks, which measure urban productivity in terms of jobs and economic output and widgets or services exchanged, to include a different question? What if, along with providing us with a place to live and work, our cities also provided us with the essential ingredient we can't survive without—food?

I suspect that just asking the question will force us to look deeply at the definitional divide we've constructed between the urban and the rural. And the philosophical heart of that divide lies,

I think, in our attitude toward the land itself—the land being the literal soil on which we build our notions of what properly belongs. We're entirely comfortable with the idea of the rural landscape as a working *land*scape, the soil from which our food comes, the place where we negotiate productive effort with, and from, the earth. The city, on the other hand, is a landscape in which the *land* is little more than backdrop or platform for activities that aren't intrinsically connected to it and don't grow from it. Even urban places that don't seem to fit this argument—parks and green spaces, for example—are either appreciated for the passive recreational opportunities they offer or, at worst, merely tolerated as long as they don't get in the way of more important efforts of city building. (One can see the latter in the approach that many cities take with regard to community gardens, where people come together to grow food. The gardens are often considered to be temporary land uses until a "better," "more appropriate" purpose can be found for the space.)

Closely connected to this conceptual divide between urban and rural is our attitude to nature. Nature exists "out there," untouched by humans. Cultivation is a corruption of the pristine.

46

Reimagining our cities as places of food production encourages us to be guided by a different ethic, an ethic of productive possibility. It asks us to work the land—growing with it and from it—and to work with natural systems. It asks us to see the city as a living landscape, its soil generative of value precisely for what it is: something alive, something from which much goodness can grow.

three

PRODUCTIVE POSSIBILITY

THE OLDER FELLOW who lives in an apartment above a popular café at the end of my street, on a busy commercial corner, is one of the most productive urban food-growers I've ever met. In a space that consists of a parking pad for three cars, a fenced-in square of soil 10 feet by 10 feet, and a small outdoor deck on the second floor, he manages to grow more vegetables than I could eat in a year.

His arsenal consists of buckets lined up in tight rows against every edge of the property. I tried to count the gleaming white plastic containers (the kind bulk food comes in) and lost track just short of 100. When I asked him about the volume, he shrugged and said, "I used to do more."

The containers may look unconventional, but they don't look messy—they're too purposeful for that. Filled with soil, each bucket contains a plant—tomato, pepper, eggplant, or some other vegetable—and sometimes there's also a bean plant winding up the stake. The chain-link fencing around the property is likewise covered by midsummer with the green leaves of bean plants; a trellis behind the parking pad supports lush zucchinis. Off to the side of the car area, where there is a small square of soil, a fig tree spreads its tropical-looking foliage over in-ground plantings of eggplant, mint, basil, lettuce, peas, onions, and more. He eats a lot of salad, he tells me, and he makes vats of tomato sauce, freezes extra produce, and gives away plenty.

He's out there most days, but I've noticed that, aside from watering, his work in the garden consists mainly of hanging around and chatting with the dozens of people who stop by. "It kills the time in summer," he said when I complimented him on the garden. "It's something to do." I suspect that the food-growing traditions of his Portuguese heritage have something to do with it as well.

Maybe it's his daily presence that protects his garden—that, and his vigilance. There's something about his stance and demeanor—stocky and a little gruff, his ruddy face slow to smile—that seems to broadcast a "don't mess with my planting" message. I've never seen any evidence of vandalism. What I have seen, though, is evidence of ingenuity. For one, a lack of soil—a "yard" that is three-quarters driveway, for example—is not an insurmountable barrier to food growing. Simple buckets can be surprisingly bountiful. For another, double-duty tricks maximize production: tomato stakes moonlight as bean poles, fences function as valuable vertical supports that call out for a vine or three. And finally, the harvest of one crop makes way for the planting of another: empty space left over from the early lettuce provides room for a second crop of beets or basil.

"Next year, I'll show you my tricks," he offers.

URBAN FOOD PRODUCTION is not, despite often being perceived as such, an anomalous activity embraced by only a small percentage of the population—garden keeners like my neighbor with a hankering for fresh vegetables and the luxury of leisure time in which to indulge their hobby. It is, in fact, surprisingly widespread. The Food and Agriculture Organization (FAO) of the United Nations, for example, estimates that more than 100 million people worldwide derive direct income from urban farming. In terms of consumption rather than employment, a 1996 study from the United Nations Development Programme estimates that 800 million urban farmers and gardeners produce 15 percent of all the food consumed on the planet. As well, nearly 70 percent of global commercial egg production comes from poultry raised in or close to cities.

Though most of this global urban agricultural activity takes place in developing countries, there is also a high proportion of food grown in North American urban areas. According to a recent research report called *Health Benefits of Urban Agriculture,* by Anne Bellows, Katherine Brown, and Jac Smit of the Community Food Security Coalition, "One third of the 2 million farms in the United States alone are located within metropolitan areas, and produce 35% of U.S. vegetables, fruit, livestock, poultry, and fish." Statistics Canada reports that there are more than 35,000 farms (15.5 percent of the total) within the country's metropolitan areas. The Greater Vancouver Regional District, for example, produces 27 percent of British Columbia's gross farm receipts. This is not as incongruous as it sounds when you consider that, historically, cities often sprang up on the best farmland, with production close to the market ensuring that the urban population could be fed. (Michael Olson, in his 1994 book *MetroFarm,* makes a surprising point regarding American cities: "According to a recent Census of Agriculture, the most productive farmland in the United States is in the Borough of the Bronx! The second most productive farmland is in the City of San Francisco!")

If some of the best farmland in North America exists below and adjacent to urban centers, it should come as no surprise that city food gardens can be enormously productive. To be sure, it often takes a great deal of effort to return urban soil to some semblance of health, given the indignities to which it has been subjected. The parking pad where my neighbor grows all that food could hardly be considered farmland (you'd need to go back a century or more to find any trace of agricultural memory on that spot), but through creativity and ingenuity he has developed a garden that could go up against any farm within 50 miles and be in the running for the productivity prize.

Counterintuitive as it may sound, urban food gardens are often more productive—in terms of the ratio between food yield and size of space—than their rural agricultural counterparts. In other words, far from being unable to feed ourselves (at least partially, and possibly significantly) from our small urban plots, we can in fact generate a prodigious amount of food. One of my more benign and harmless diversions is to collect stories and statistics on macho food production—stories of the people who have managed to grow outrageous amounts of food on their small city plots; statistics of what's possible. (In all honesty, I should confess that I don't think of this as a hobby. It's more like an addiction to urban ag porn . . .) And such stories never fail to inspire and titillate.

The writer Barbara Kingsolver is the queen of my list, though I'm being a sneaky cheat by including her, since she and her family grow their food on a farm in the country not in the city. Still, their food-growing experiment—living for a year on the food they produced themselves—is hugely instructive. And equally exhaustion-inducing, since they appear to have done little else for a year than toil in their vegetable patch. In her wonderful 2007 book *Animal, Vegetable, Miracle*—just one of her many wonderful

50

books—Kingsolver describes how her family of four grew all of their produce on 3,524 square feet of garden beds. That works out to just 40 feet by 22 feet per person—smaller than the typical urban yard, I'm guessing. (Kingsolver wryly notes that "it felt a lot bigger when we were weeding it.") The family's main off-farm purchases for the year were organic grain for animal feed and 300 pounds of flour for bread making. Other than that, they basically lived on each hard-won bite grown from that 3,524 square feet of soil. The family's food footprint for the year was, she calculates, somewhere around one acre.

The kicker, of course, is that this little exercise in fruit and vegetable production consumed most of their lives—or it sounds that way, at least, in her delightful telling. If you share her dream of extreme self-sufficiency in the food department, read her book *before* you plunk down money on the farm—you just might slump away, tired at the thought of all that gardening work. (One small corner of my self-sufficiency daydream she didn't deflate, though, concerns cheese-making. I plan to spend next winter following her lead and turning my kitchen into a dairy. She makes homemade cream cheese and mozzarella sound very simple, and very tasty, indeed.)

What I found most revealing about Kingsolver's story is not the time she needed to spend in order to eat off her land, but the relatively tiny amount of space in which it was possible. Others have found much the same thing. According to R.J. Ruppenthal's book *Fresh Food from Small Spaces*, published in 2008, "Most urban residents can learn to grow as much as 10 to 20 percent of the fresh food their families eat from an average-sized urban condominium or apartment space. Those with a backyard or larger patio can do even better." *The Backyard Homestead* (2009), edited by Carleen Madigan, suggests that "A quarter-acre lot, planned out well and cultivated intensively, can produce most of the food for a small family," and estimates yields of 2,000-plus pounds of vegetables from a quarter-acre lot. Even those without in-ground growing space can get impressive yields: "you can grow as many as 15 pounds of tomatoes from just one self-watering container on the back patio."

If all these numbers and stats seem a bit, well, theoretical rather than *lived,* here are some results from people walking the talk. In the late 1990s, a group of seniors in Toronto growing vegetables at the Frances Beavis Community Garden divided 1,000 square feet of land into twenty-six plots. One of the gardeners grew more than 35 kilograms of vegetables—pak choy, amaranth, spinach, hairy gourd, and more—in her 3½-square-meter plot. The Dervaes family of Pasadena, California, had even more dramatic results. In 2002, they decided to grow more vegetables and fewer flowers in their front yard and backyard. The first year, they harvested 2,500 pounds; the second year, 3,500 pounds; the third year, 6,000 pounds. All this—350 different types of vegetables, herbs, edible flowers, fruits, and berries, grown organically—from one-tenth of an acre. (The film *HomeGrown* documents their adventure.)

My favorite story of inspiring fecundity, though, comes from Chris Thoreau, a British Columbian gardener and urban agriculture activist. In 2008, Thoreau harvested more than 800 pounds of squash from one Vancouver yard—and passed it along to a local community center.

Of course, things don't work out so productively for everyone. Brooklyn writer Manny Howard tells the disastrous story of his experiment in subsistence farming in that city in a 2007 *New York Magazine* article. Soil tests revealed that his 20-foot-by-40-foot backyard plot was loaded with lead, so he had 5½ tons of topsoil trucked in from a Long Island farm, at great expense. Just as his

> Maximizing Space

O N SMALL urban lots, the gardener's lament, *if only I had more room*, takes on added urgency. One way to maximize yield in minimal space is to plant in layers, making use of the productive potential beyond ground level: tucking fruit-bearing shrubs under nut trees, for example, and shade-tolerant herbs and salad greens under the shrubs.

> Tree (or canopy) layer: fruit trees, edible nut trees
> Smaller tree layer: serviceberries, pawpaws
> Shrub layer: currants, gooseberries, blueberries, raspberries, elderberries
> Vine layer: grapes, kiwis
> Perennial layer: mint, rhubarb
> Annual layer: arugula, lettuce
> Groundcover layer: strawberries, creeping thyme
> Soil layer: potatoes, carrots, daikon, parsnips

garden was starting to provide him with food, an August tornado flattened his crops and splintered the roof of his chicken coop. His rabbits failed to reproduce like rabbits, and after taking them to a stud farm to do the deed, the mother rabbit killed all her baby bunnies. By the end of the summer, his garden had managed to feed him for only three weeks—a string of meals he characterized as monotonous. He'd spent $11,000 and lost 29 pounds.

As return on the investment goes, most gardeners do a lot better than Howard did. Indeed, it's hard to imagine a household purchase that costs less than seeds. For a couple of bucks, you can fill the backyard with bounty. It's interesting to note that even the 2009 White House food garden represented a cash outlay of only $200— and that's a garden where, presumably, no expense was spared. (I suspect that the veggie patch was the cheapest infrastructure improvement that place has seen in a long time.) Regular folks tend to spend even less. According to the American-based National Gardening Association, the average amount of money spent on U.S. food gardens in 2008 was US$70 per food-growing household. (The NGA also reports that 36 million households, or 31 percent of the total in the U.S., participated in food gardening in 2008. The number was expected to increase by 19 percent in 2009, with 43 million households planning to grow food that year.)

Whether or not we value our food gardens in monetary terms and translate each pound of tomatoes into cold hard dollars, there's no doubt that our backyard food represents money saved. The more intensively we pack the plants in, and the more carefully we plan our crop rotations (filling in harvested spaces with succession plantings), the higher the production and the higher the value.

For those who want to make it a full-time endeavor, and a commercial one to boot, there's the SPIN-Gardening model. The acronym stands for "small plot intensive," and it's a growing

54

system developed by Wally Satzewich and Gail Vandersteen of Saskatchewan. It's a proprietary system, so you need to purchase the manuals they publish in order to learn the details of their method, but the basic idea is simple enough: by growing only high-value niche-market crops such as spinach, radishes, and lettuce, and using intensive crop rotation, you can make a lot of money from an urban plot that's less than an acre in size. Satzewich figures $50,000 profit from half an acre. His numbers were tested by the Institute for Innovations in Local Farming, which was cofounded by Roxanne Christensen, who is Satzewich and Vandersteen's SPIN farming partner. The institute, which has since closed, operated Somerton Tanks Demonstration Farm (also closed) in northeast Philadelphia, which served as the U.S. test bed for the SPIN method. In 2003, the farm produced $26,000 in gross sales from just half an acre; in 2006, the last year of operation, gross sales reached $68,000. "The agricultural experts told us we were crazy," says Christensen of the $50,000 goal from half an acre, "but we got there in just three years."

One of the more interesting aspects of SPIN (aside from the obvious—that they've developed a commercially successful system for integrating vegetable farming into the urban environment) is that it provides a way to hop over the two barriers obstructing widespread commercial food production in cities: the access to land problem and the access to start-up capital problem. SPIN farmers are colonizers, but with permission. They seek out back- and front yards from owners who are willing to rent their space for a small fee, or sometimes just in exchange for a share of the produce. Ward Teulon, who runs a company in Vancouver called City Farm Boy, has a dozen mini-farms around the city in people's backyards and front yards—and one on a rooftop at a condo development. He sells the produce at farmers' markets and to the more than thirty customers who have bought "garden shares" and receive regular deliveries. The people who lend him their land do so for a variety of reasons: "Some because they think urban farming is a good idea; others because they're spending money to cut weeds down and I'm offering them a way to turn a liability into something positive," says Teulon. He doesn't pay rent for the spaces, but he does give the landowners vegetables—"to keep everyone happy." When I talked with Teulon in the late fall of 2009, he was poring over seed catalogs, planning for next year's urban crops and some new adventures: distributing mushroom logs in some of the shadier, cooler yards he farms and setting up some beehives ("I hope to have hives all over the city," he enthuses).

Jean Snow and Bob Kropla are preparing for their third year of SPIN farming in Dartmouth, Nova Scotia, in a handful of neighborhood yards, including one at a group home. With 2,800 square feet ("It seemed to be bigger than that," sighs Jean, as she explains that her backyard was basically a crop of rocks before she started growing vegetables), the couple grew enough food in 2009 to supply thirteen members of their Community Shared Agriculture project with salad greens, beans, peas, tomatoes, beets, carrots, potatoes, onions, and more. "We don't have any problems finding customers," says Jean, "and we don't have any problems finding land. People come to us."

Shannon Lee Stirling is likewise replete with borrowed land. As project coordinator for Backyard Bounty, she farms thirty residential yards in Guelph, Ontario. The first time we spoke on the phone, she had just come in from "working the fields," as she put it in true farmer fashion. It's only later, when I tour those fields with her, that the incongruity of the term sinks in. City buses rather than tractors roll past her "fields," pets rather than wildlife are the creatures of her farm lots, driveways rather than hedgerows border her crops, and tidy urban houses frame the agricultural view.

"I've been a gardening geek from the time I was a kid," says Shannon as we visit a dozen of the yards she and her Backyard Bounty colleagues cultivate throughout the city. It quickly becomes clear that Shannon is a scrounger—someone always on the lookout for useful materials that others have discarded or are not using. She scoops fallen apples from the ground and snacks on them during our visit. She points out the dumpster where she scavenged cast-off palettes to build a chicken coop. She spies wooden grape crates out by a curb and talks about returning later with a truck to collect them. But the main thing she collects is yards: "I'm looking for people who feel that their yards could go to a better, more productive use than lawn."

Of the homeowners who answered Backyard Bounty's call for space in 2009 (including a Guelph city councillor, whose garden Backyard Bounty filled with zucchini), Shannon is full of praise: "Our homeowners are amazing." What they get out of the deal is a small percentage of the produce and someone else to look after their yard. "We've only had one problem so far," says Shannon as she takes me to a large front yard filled with neat rows of tomatoes, zucchinis, beans, and eggplants. It's the home of an older woman who can no longer garden but who loves looking out her front window to see the space put to good use. "The neighbors weren't at all happy," says Shannon. "They were ready to start a petition." A strategic application of straw mulch between the rows calmed the neighborhood storm.

When I ask Shannon if Backyard Bounty has managed to make enough money to be worth the effort, she sighs, gives a bit of a shrug, and says, "It's our first year of business *and* we're farmers..." Further comment is unnecessary. But it's clear that she's in it for more than the promise of eventual financial reward. She's spreading the word about the ultimate scrounge—space for food: "I always tell potential homeowner participants, 'The best reason we're not food-gardening your yard is because you are.'"

AS AN INFORMAL, non-commercial expression of communality, backyard sharing has a long tradition, and in the last couple of years it has experienced quite a growth spurt. Considering that almost half of the North American population does not live in single-unit detached housing where the yard space is unambiguously theirs, it's not surprising that many people yearn for room to grow and have developed creative ways to find it.

Take this posting, for example, which appeared on the Toronto Urban Growers website in the summer of 2009, soon after the group had formed and gone live with a website: "I have a big backyard. Does anyone want to farm it for me? We can share the yield, I can provide the water." So simple, so open and trusting, so collaborative and willing to give and take. I'd even go so far as to say that this short posting encapsulates a lot of what we would hope to find in our communities: a spirit of exchange, informal and negotiable. Unlike so many property exchanges, with every inch getting vetted in a legalistic framework, this one seems unconcerned with liability issues and responsibility fears and all the things that could go wrong when two people enter into an agreement. Instead, and yes, possibly naively, this one simply says: I've got something of value . . . wanna share?

Fred Dale, the *Toronto Star*'s gardening columnist for thirty years, wrote an article published in the *New York Times* in 1972, about a Toronto woman, Mrs. Beatrice Fischer, who had a large property in North Toronto and offered two acres of the space to local apartment dwellers. Her gardening invitation was printed in the *Star*'s social column and within ten days seventy requests had flowed in to the newspaper. A successful applicant for one of the twenty-six plots was a woman who explained that she wanted a space in which to garden because her son thought tomatoes grew underground, like potatoes.

The internet has simplified the logistics of backyard sharing and facilitated its development. The nonprofit LifeCycles Project Society, of Victoria, B.C., has been a pioneer in capturing the potential of the Web to connect gardeners' desires with gardeners' spaces. In 2006, they developed a computer program—a mapping tool—for backyard sharing, and they provide the technology for free to groups and individuals who are interested in coordinating the project in various cities across North America. From the first year, in which three cities were involved, they've grown to having thirty partner organizations using the program, from Halifax, Nova Scotia, to San Diego, California—and one as far away as New Zealand. "We're franchising, basically," says Christopher Hawkins, the project leader of LifeCycles' Sharing Backyards Initiative. He explains that LifeCycles originally started the project in an effort to find gardening space for people who couldn't get a plot in Victoria's community gardens. "There's a waiting list for every community garden in town, and the wait times can be long because people tend to give up their plots only if they move out of town or they die. We started Sharing Backyards to take that pressure off."

The computer program doesn't currently track figures on the number of people who have successfully made a garden match or on the amount of land shared, but when Hawkins and I spoke in the fall of 2009 there were 369 yards on offer, including a 40-acre plot. "The number of yards being shared has grown exponentially," he says. "People snap them up."

Though some potential participants offering land might be worried that their hospitality will be abused, Hawkins knows of only one story of a match gone bad. "I heard about someone who put a lot of effort into the garden and then the homeowner sold the place without telling them and the gardener lost all their work." But Hawkins wonders if this story is in fact true: "I've heard the exact same story a couple of times but the place it supposedly happened changes each time."

It takes a lot of trust to freely advertise in cyberspace your willingness to invite a stranger into your yard and your life. A nonprofit organization in Toronto, the Stop Community Food Centre, has taken the backyard-sharing concept into less anonymous territory with its Yes In My Back Yard program. Acting as a kind of broker, the Stop, instead of a computer program, does the people-connecting in one west-end community of Toronto.

At a meeting held in September 2009 to launch the project, roughly thirty neighborhood residents showed up. As we munched on damson plums and cookies (food organizations can be counted on to provide good snacks at their meetings), the organizers asked us to introduce ourselves to the people sitting beside us and find out their favorite vegetables. My seatmates and I were stumped by the challenge—we settled on "anything fresh." This little ice-breaking exercise had an immediate, focusing effect: soon everyone was talking about food and dreaming of the goodies we might produce in someone else's backyard.

What struck me most was the casual intimacy of the exchanges. With just a few simple sentences, we revealed so much. And what was expressed most often was a yearning for something missing or lost. Krysten, for example, mentioned that she lived in a condo and so was looking for gardening space—nothing surprising in that, and yet when she added that she came "from a long line of farmers," it was clear that the idea of her own garden touched a deeper chord. Rosemary talked of the freshly picked asparagus she tasted on her honeymoon, years ago, and how her yard was too shady to grow it. Ginny told us that she had recently moved from a house to an apartment and no longer had a garden—"I miss that, a lot." (Ginny also inspired us with her story of successfully growing four large tomato plants in her apartment that summer. She missed her garden but she was doing everything possible to create a new one, including an impressive effort at indoor growing.)

Another fellow, Paul, had an unusual offering for the group: a renter, he didn't own his backyard but he'd asked his landlord about gardening it and, with permission granted, was now happy to proffer the space that wasn't his to someone else. As a musician who travels a lot, Paul wouldn't even be around to share in the bounty. He just liked the idea of facilitating a productive transfer.

Wolf, an older gentleman, described his yard as "overgrown with oaks," but thought that someone in the neighborhood might be able to find slivers of sunlight and grow food in containers. Janet energized us all with her enticing gift: in her large backyard, she was growing more food than she could cope with on her own. She was looking for someone to help eat it and preserve it, sharing in the canning, sharing in the food.

The mood in the room was one of opportunity, and the spirit of conviviality didn't dampen a bit when Liz Curran, the Stop's Yes in My Back Yard coordinator, started to outline some of the trickier details of the sharing arrangements. "We'll do our best at helping out with the initial process," Liz said, "but once a match is made, it's up to each pair to come up with their own common understanding, and each situation will be different."

The questions each pair would need to address ranged from the practical to the more philosophical, with financial considerations always lurking in the corners. Who would pay for any soil improvements? At first it seemed obvious that the gardener borrowing the land should, but then doubt set in: after all, soil amendments would be of a more permanent nature, benefiting the land lender, so maybe the cost should be shared. What about water? Should the gardener contribute to the expense of metered water? How would the gardener's cultivation methods affect the yard owner and vice versa? Would both agree to organic cultivation, right down to the details of what the term organic means? (For example, would commercial fertilizers be okay?) How would the produce be shared: 60/40, 70/30? And perhaps the thorniest question, in the early days of getting to know each other anyway: how would privacy and security considerations be dealt with? Was the homeowner giving access to the gardener alone or also to a partner, kids, and friends? Would the homeowner's bathroom be included in the sharing deal? What if the gardener was growing food to sell? Would the homeowner be okay with commercial use of their land?

In the end, there were no one-size-fits-all answers. As Liz Curran had suggested, it all came down to what the partners would feel comfortable with and how they wanted to negotiate their arrangement. The details would vary. The important thing was to sort them out up front.

An interesting dynamic developed as we discussed the potential sticking points of backyard sharing. Ideas on how to take the project further started to gel. Janet told us of her brother's horse farm and how, if we organized a truck, we could access free manure. Rosemary suggested that we compile a roster of people willing to maintain gardens while the gardeners were away on summer holidays. Natalie volunteered to organize a hands-on workshop for participants in her yard, with training in how to prepare a garden bed for vegetable planting. There was talk of a community message board on which to post questions. The Stop floated the idea of a tool-lending library. In short, the often-hidden resources that exist within any group were being made available in a spirit of goodwill problem-solving—we were turning into a little community with a shared and positive purpose.

For those who are hesitant to branch out with strangers, there's always friends and family. As I confessed in chapter 1, I am a garden colonizer, always on the lookout for growing opportunities, especially now that I've jam-packed my own garden space. I built a pond at my sister's house, 30 miles away, just for the experimental experience of growing native water plants. I developed a tall-grass prairie in an old agricultural field at my ex-partner's father's country property (and presumptuously called it a birthday present), not only for the chance to nurture some rare prairie plants but also so I could indulge my pyromaniac tendencies with an annual prairie burn. But my most meaningful, and now bittersweet, backyard sharing experience was the garden I grew at my dad's house in the last summer of his life.

Although he had grown tomatoes for decades, my dad was by that point beyond capable of such effort. There would be no more poring over the heritage seed catalogs, no more seedlings lined up on shelving he'd constructed for the sunny front window, no more lists describing the dozens of heritage varieties he was growing—lists that he distributed to people who had, as he put it, done him neighborly favors over the past year and whom he invited to choose as many plants, from as many different varieties, as they wanted. His deliveries were quite a sight: a van full of tall, leggy plants, scooting around town, these ones for his favorite bank teller, those for his barbershop quartet buddies. His was a plant-sharing mission on overdrive.

> Vegetables That Can Be Grown in Part Shade

GROWING FOOD in the city often requires more than a little ingenuity—rarely is the urban gardener working with ideal conditions. For example, buildings, houses, and trees may block access to sunlight, creating shady spots that are tough to use for growing vegetables. While tomatoes might be out of the question in such situations, there are plenty of edible plants that will do well in part shade. Here are a few:

> arugula   > parsnips   > peas

> beets   > spinach   > parsley

> kale   > radishes   > rhubarb

> lettuce   > garlic

....

My mission of backyard garden sharing was much more modest. I planted blackberry canes along my dad's back fence and a couple of Moon and Stars heritage watermelon plants in the middle of his lawn. Whenever I went to the hospital to visit him that last summer, I always stopped by the house to water and weed the plantings. My brothers lived next door and helped out, one being careful to mow around the plants when he cut the lawn, the other carving watermelon platforms out of spare wood, so the fruit wouldn't rest on the ground and rot.

The growth of the plants marked time for me in an otherwise out-of-time, suspended summer spent waiting, worrying, and doing what I could to cushion the inevitable. One of the few moments of pure joy occurred, with welcome surprise, when I was poking around in the big watermelon leaves and discovered a melon the size of a clenched fist hiding beneath. I focused all my emotional energy on that fruit for the next few weeks, checking that it was securely resting on its wooden platform, pinching off the flowers from the rest of the plant to direct its resources to that growing fist, watering to the point of flood. When I picked the melon (its skin all star-speckled, just as its name indicated) and took it to the hospital, we turned that antiseptically green room into the sunniest of summer picnics, letting the juice run from rind to chin, unfazed by the delicious mess.

As for the blackberry canes, which spread prodigiously, the people who now live in the house have cut them down. But you need heavier machinery than a weed whacker to suppress blackberries, I've discovered. A few new canes continue to sprout every year and, when I visit my brothers next door, I peek at their progress. And sometimes steal a berry or ten. I figure the neighbors won't mind sharing.

65

four

HARVESTING SPACE

THIRTY YEARS AGO, Michael Levenston set out to answer a basic question. Levenston had just recently cofounded, with Bob Woodsworth, an organization called City Farmer—a nonprofit group that the two environmental activists and energy researchers cheekily subtitled "Canada's Office of Urban Agriculture." They didn't worry that the "office" was in fact a heavily contaminated vacant lot beside a working railway line in a residential area of Vancouver. It sounded official, and what better way to muster credibility than by starting out with an authoritative, if inflated, descriptive tag?

In the early days of such an organization, some people might have been content to spread the word about what the then relatively new concept of urban agriculture actually meant. Along with that, though, Levenston set his sights on an even more visionary goal: he wanted to know what urban agriculture could *achieve* in a large North American city like Vancouver. To find out, Levenston did some number crunching. He calculated that the combined area of back- and front yards, boulevards, and vacant lots in the city equaled 6,515 acres, or 283,793,400 square feet of potential growing space ready for planting. He then considered various estimates of the amount of space needed to grow enough vegetables for a family of four. The figures ranged from a high of 2,400 square feet to a low of 1,000 square feet; Levenston settled on the highest, and thus most conservative, number. Recognizing that not every bit of available land could be enlisted in food production, he extracted for his calculation just 50 percent of the back- and front yard space, 10 percent of the boulevards, and 10 percent of the open spaces in public rights of way to come up with the 6,515-acre figure. He did not include parks, cemeteries, or the grounds of schools, churches, and hospitals. He also subtracted 10 percent for areas too shady to grow vegetables and 2 percent for paths, and was astonished to discover that "the city of Vancouver has enough land available so that its inhabitants [a population at the time of 427,000] can grow all their own vegetables within city limits." Indeed, more than they need, "with some to spare."

Even without doing the math, it's easy to find umpteen examples of places in our cities that have food-growing potential that is currently squandered. Of course, "squandered" is a loaded term—one person's "wasted" patch of grass on a boulevard might be another person's ideal dog-walking destination. Such judgements depend on the lens through which we filter our notions of value. So let's avoid the controversy of competing demands and consider only those urban areas that are vacant or abandoned.

Detroit, Philadelphia, and Buffalo—northeastern cities with a strong industrial heritage—are some of the places that first come to mind in any discussion of the pervasive problem of abandoned, vacant land in North American cities. As the manufacturing base has eroded, these cities have been left with a legacy of unused, sometimes toxic, land. The scope of the problem is enormous.

Detroit, for example—perhaps the poster child in this unfortunate accounting—has approximately 100,000 parcels of abandoned property within the city limits, for a combined total of 40 square miles, or about one-third of the city's land. Dan Pitera, an associate professor of architecture at the University of Detroit Mercy, points out that the amount of empty land in Detroit approximates the total land mass of San Francisco. This inventory of vacant land is accompanied by an estimated 24,000 empty buildings, about a quarter of which are candidates for demolition at the city's expense.

Philadelphia, the sixth largest city in the U.S., is another community struggling with the problem of abandoned properties. According to a working paper produced by Jerry Kaufman and Martin Bailkey for the Lincoln Institute of Land Policy in 2000, there are approximately 30,900 vacant parcels in Philadelphia, 31 percent of which are publicly owned and thus represent a significant liability concern. It costs millions annually just to clear and maintain a portion of these vacant properties, so they are a direct drain on the public purse.

Not only do tax-delinquent lands burden cities financially and administratively, but they also project an image of decline. Milwaukee may be a fabulous city (personally, I love the place—it's a hotbed of front-yard prairie naturalization and for that alone I find it inspiring), but with 4 percent of the city's total land area (or 2,500 acres of public and private property) vacant, any image of prosperity is somewhat tarnished. Likewise, Chicago, a city that prides itself on its can-do attitude, hasn't quite done it yet. With an estimated 70,000 vacant lots, there's room (and need) for at least 70,000 improvements.

ABOUT SEVEN YEARS ago, I attended the American Community Gardening Association's conference in Chicago and for the closing night's dinner we ate al fresco in what had, just a few months

69

earlier, been a vacant lot. It was a picnic hosted by City Farm, a Chicago-based urban agriculture project run by the nonprofit organization Resource Center, and it was in not just any vacant lot, but one bordering Cabrini-Green—Chicago's pioneering, and notorious, experiment in social housing. Some of the Cabrini-Green towers have since been demolished, but on that night they loomed over a different sort of pioneering (and anything but notorious) experiment in urban farming. City Farm had turned the vacant lot, where dozens of us now milled around, snacking on grilled vegetable kebabs and salads, into an acre of productive growing space. As dusk settled, the lights from Chicago's downtown Loop glowed in the near distance, and we wandered through row upon row of abundance. More than eighty varieties of vegetables flourished in the space—towering tomatoes (twenty-five different heirloom varieties), peppers, okra, beets, kale—all testament to the nourishing power of compost, 2 feet of which had been piled on top of an impermeable layer of clay, which in turn had been piled on top of building demolition waste.

The feast was delicious, the mood celebratory, and we marveled at the unlikeliness of it all: warmed by the August night air, we were picnicking at an epicenter of urban contrast, with the poverty of Cabrini-Green to one side, the wealth of Chicago's Gold Coast to the other, and the lights of the downtown Loop's skyscrapers bathing the sky in front of us. The scene couldn't have been more urban, and yet we were surrounded by an acre of vegetables growing on top of rubble. Maybe there's something about contradiction that heightens the senses, but rarely have I felt so alert to urban possibility.

The contrasts evident at Chicago's City Farm go beyond its location; they're also built into its structure. Organic waste collected from restaurants, police horse stables, and local landscapers is the building block for the resource of compost. Volunteer labor makes possible the prodigious volume (15,000 pounds of produce) and the significant economic return (US$60,000 worth of produce sold annually). Customers are at once the highest of high-end restaurants (the prestigious North Pond Restaurant, for example) and people at the lower end of the economic scale (local social housing residents are charged less for the produce sold at City Farm's markets, while restaurants pay market value). University professors volunteering their time work alongside youth interns who are learning about sustainable agriculture and receiving basic job training.

Perhaps the biggest contrast and contradiction, though, is contained in the term "vacant land." Maybe the phrase is, in fact, a misnomer. Land is hardly vacant, even when "empty." It is instead occupied by soil, and every bit of soil represents growing potential. That is what City Farm has harnessed; that is the idea they harvest. "There are huge possibilities," says Tim Wilson, the director of urban agriculture for Resource Center. "We can provide three jobs per vacant acre and grow 25,000 pounds of produce per acre." In other words, potential is what they see: "The city of Chicago would like us to tend all vacant properties," says Ken Dunn, founder and executive director of Resource Center. "Every vacant lot ought to be greened and improved. We clean up, improve and protect the property at no cost to the city; the city provides the property at no cost to the group." Just imagine: 70,000 possible farms, urban decline turned to urban growth.

Projects like City Farm always make me think of Edgar Allan Poe's story "The Purloined Letter." In that tale, a stolen letter is "hidden" in plain view. Obscured by its obviousness, no one can see or find the letter because it is staring them right in the face. The parallel with vacant land (perhaps better called land in limbo) is not much of a stretch. Usually considered a problem in economically depressed urban areas, the land exists as a resource precisely where fresh, inexpensive and readily accessible food is most needed. The solution is thus contained in the very term used to describe the problem: vacant land is . . . *available*. And nowhere is it more available than in Detroit.

MY INTRODUCTION TO Detroit, when I was eleven years old, was somewhat incongruous and less than auspicious. The city accidentally became the first stop on a three-week-long road trip my dad and I were taking from southern Ontario to the Grand Canyon. I was nervous and excited about the adventure, very aware of the long list of *never before's* I was diving into: I'd never before been out of Canada, seen a big city, traveled with my dad, read a map . . . And there I was, the navigator, sort of. It all felt very adult, even if the decisions I was making were firmly planted in childhood. (Turn here, I'd direct, angling for a detour to the Flintstones theme park . . .)

Our planned early morning departure for the trip slid into midday, and the border took longer than expected, so we only got as far as Detroit that first night when it became too dark to continue driving. The thing is, this was a *camping* trip. My introduction to the big scary Motor City was thus from the pop-up tent top of an orange VW camper van. At daybreak the next morning, I looked out the screened windows of the van's tent top and thought, can this really be, that we're *camping in Detroit?*

Almost four decades later, in the autumn of 2009, I was back in Detroit, with that same sense of incongruous adventure, though this time my question was agricultural rather than vacational: can this really be, that people are *farming in Detroit?*

There are many things for which Detroit is known—its automobile manufacturing, its Motown music, its crime rate, its disparity between rich and poor, its racial tensions—but in the past few years, it has become recognized for something entirely new. Detroit has become a mecca for urban agriculture enthusiasts from across North America, and indeed the world, who are curious to see how this depleted urban giant has been transforming itself into a center for city farming. (A joke making the rounds of Detroit's urban agriculture activists is that someone should make a movie of all the film crews flocking to the city to make documentaries about Detroit's urban farms.)

It's not hard to see why the narrative possibilities of Detroit's growing transformation appeal to documentarians. This was the ur-city of industrialization, ground zero of the car. Now, with the automobile industry on life support, it has also become the ur-city of post-industrial blight and flight, poster child for urban decline. Drive through its neighborhoods and the signs of shrinking prospects are everywhere. Boarded-up buildings look positively hopeful compared to the burned-out, collapsing structures that surround them—at least the houses, offices, and stores with plywood over their doors and windows are still standing.

But there are other signs to read in this landscape. Look closely at what appears to be a field of tall grass beside an empty house with craters in its roof, and you might see that the grass is not grass at all, but rather . . . onions. Detroit is becoming a *farmed* city. And it is teeming with city farmers.

With major automakers in bailout mode, Detroit suffers from high unemployment and foreclosure rates. One-third of its 800,000 citizens now live in poverty, making it one of the most impoverished major cities in the United States. The evidence of hardship is written on the very fabric of the city in the form of 40 square miles of vacant lots.

But there's another kind of evidence visible in Detroit. More than 800 of those vacant lots have been turned into gardens and mini-farms, producing food for people in need. And Detroit is full to bursting with people and groups committed to expanding that number each year. The Garden Resource Program Collaborative, for example, a coalition of groups including the Detroit Agriculture Network and the Greening of Detroit, has teamed up to provide access to resources and educational opportunities for anyone interested in food gardening—whether at schools, with community groups, or in backyards. Urban Farming, an international nonprofit organization headquartered in Detroit, has partnered with locals to create more than fifty gardens at schools and churches and on unused land.

Through the Detroit Collaborative Design Center he runs at the University of Detroit Mercy, Dan Pitera is exploring the possibility of transforming not just vacant lots but also vacant buildings into urban farming projects, repurposing buildings as greenhouses, for example. "We're looking at not just transplanting a rural farm in the city, but rather utilizing the existing infrastructure in creative ways that really make urban farms unique. Detroit could reinvent what it means to be a world-class city," says Pitera, "and it should include things like urban farming."

Other groups are doing hard work at the policy level as well. The Detroit Black Community Food Security Network, a coalition of organizations and individuals, successfully urged the city to form the Detroit Food Policy Council and drafted a clear set of actions needed to create a "food secure" Detroit in which "all of its citizens are hunger-free, healthy and benefit from the food systems that impact their lives." One of the recommendations is that the city support efforts to identify and turn into production those acres and acres of vacant land.

In some ways, it's not surprising that Detroit is such a hotbed of urban agriculture. Not only is the need so great, but it's also a city with innovative historic precedents related to food growing. During the depression of the 1890s, for example, Detroit mayor Hazen S. Pingree initiated and expanded a number of social programs, including one colloquially called the "potato patch plans," or "Pingree's Potato Patches." He urged vacant lot owners to allow those who were unemployed (roughly 25,000 people, or one-tenth of the city's population) to grow food on the owners' empty lots. He urged churches to collect money for seeds and garden tools, and supplemented that call with a municipal investment of $3,000 toward program costs. In the first year, $12,000 worth of vegetables were harvested, saving the city money that it would otherwise have needed to spend on relief.

Another Detroit innovation comes from the more recent past. In the 1970s, then-mayor Coleman A. Young started a program called Farm-A-Lot, which formalized a permit system encouraging residents to farm vacant lots in their neighborhoods. A group of Detroit landlords took him literally at his word, releasing eight beef cattle and a cluster of hens on a vacant 3-acre lot a dozen blocks from Tiger Stadium. In a March 1975 Pittsburgh newspaper article, the landlords proclaimed that Detroit, with its 38,127 vacant lots equal to 10 square miles of open country, "could become one of the biggest ranches in the United States." Publicity stunts aside (the cattle were shipped back to their Oakland County farm later that day), the people of Detroit responded with enthusiasm to the program, taking advantage of the free permits and seed kits. As a result, more than 22,000 lots were farmed by the early 1980s.

One of the conditions of the Farm-A-Lot permits was that the individuals growing the food could not sell it to others. Despite the economic needs of Detroiters, the program was not intended for income generation. However, more recent Detroit initiatives are exploring precisely this possibility. At the Eastern Market, a

Detroit farmers' market that was recently revived through community effort, you can buy onions, yams, greens, and other produce proudly labeled "Grown in Detroit," through a cooperative effort started by the Garden Resource Program Collaborative. Produce from some of the city's 800 mini-farms is sold through the co-op, with the money going back to the community.

The Fair Food Network is looking at the ways that local food entrepreneurship can be a catalyst for inner-city revitalization. The foundation commissioned economist Michael H. Shuman, author of *The Small-Mart Revolution: How Local Businesses Are Beating the Global Competition,* to study the impact that a 20-percent shift in consumer spending from nonlocal to local food would have on Detroit's economy. Summarizing his findings in RSF *Quarterly* in 2008, Shuman writes, "Just this modest change could increase the city's annual economic output by nearly half a billion dollars and create more than 4,700 jobs. Were this 20-percent spending shift to occur in the five counties surrounding Detroit . . . nearly 36,000 jobs in the region would be created. To put these numbers in perspective, a regional effort focused on Detroit food businesses would cut the city's unemployment rate in half . . ."

Shuman's analysis tackles the consumer end of the equation: how we spend our food dollars. Detroit businessman John Hantz, on the other hand, is proposing a different kind of economic revitalization for Detroit: he plans to create North America's largest urban farm. His company, Hantz Farms, is currently buying up privately owned properties and negotiating with the city for the purchase of publicly owned vacant land, all in an effort to consolidate the parcels into large lots that will serve as farming "pods" throughout the city.

When I met with Matt Allen, senior vice president of Hantz Farms, and Michael Score of Michigan State University, who is doing consulting work for the company, they tell me that their first step—in a process Allen describes as "crawl, walk, run"—is to get one 30-acre pod established in 2010. As for how many pods there will eventually be, and how many acres they will cover, "at this point, we don't have an acre goal," says Allen. "We're at the crawl stage."

The crawl stage, indeed, might be one way to describe where Detroit is at right now. A city once inhabited by 1.8 million people, its population is currently less than half of that. "How do you take a large city and shrink it?" asks Allen. "If we continue to hold on to the idea of a million and a half people again, well, the macroeconomic indicators just aren't there. We have a problem *now*."

What the city also has now, in abundance, is land. And returning that land to productive use is the cornerstone of the Hantz Farms vision. "We see our farm pods as a means to end blight, help put people back to work, put land into production, connect people to nature and create a thing of beauty," says Allen. Unspoken is a question that hangs at the end of his list: what's not to like?

For Malik Yakini, chair of the Detroit Black Community Food Security Network, a few things. "I have a problem with the scale," Yakini tells me when we meet at a café near Wayne State University on a blustery autumn day. Stirring honey into his tea—and giving a laugh and a shrug, acknowledging that as a vegan about to eat vegan-contraband honey, he's not a person of absolutes—Yakini elaborates: "One-, two-, or three-acre farms that can be managed by a family or the community are empowering, but a massive farm that a corporation owns and manages can disempower communities. It can create a permanent overclass of people benefiting economically from the communities people live in."

Yakini is quick to clarify that he's not opposed to the commercialization of urban agriculture: "For this movement to be more than just a nice idea, it has to work economically. Urban agriculture can be about creating jobs and wealth, too. But the question is: how does the project help empower the community?"

When I ask Allen about the criticisms swirling around Hantz Farms, he retains his upbeat composure and enthusiasm, and praises the urban agriculture work that Detroit's many nonprofit groups are doing: "We've made a concerted effort to reach out. We continue to support the other wonderful models that exist in the community. We're not competing against them. There's lots of room for everybody."

His optimism extends even to the possibility of the Hantz Farms business model not working out: "If we fail, what's going to happen? The city will get the land back in better shape than when we started."

It's only after I leave Detroit and its fields of food—real and potential—that the irony (and Economics 101 logic) of what Hantz Farms is attempting to do finally sinks in. The company's success depends on accumulating abundant vacant land and developing it into farm pods precisely in order to make vacant land scarce—and thus valuable again. At 40 square miles in total, vacant lots are a dime a dozen, and it's not unheard of for the city to sell them off for a dollar. But buy up those thousands of acres and put them into production and the amount of land available for development decreases, at the same time as its scarcity raises its value.

Just how quickly and how assuredly any benefits trickle down to the people who currently live there is a question without a promising answer, particularly when prosperity-generation is concentrated in, and controlled by, one company.

While Hantz Farms puts its faith in Economics 101—scarcity equals value—other entrepreneurial urban agriculture projects put their faith in the logic of food-plenty.

Red Hook Community Farm in Brooklyn is one such project. That a farm grows in Brooklyn is unlikely enough. That the farm grows on asphalt doubles the surprise. That the farm is tended by neighbourhood teenagers... well, you get the idea. The project began in 2003, when Added Value, a nonprofit group that works with youth, approached the New York City Department of Parks & Recreation for permission to turn an abandoned asphalt ball field into a working farm. Employing young people from the Red Hook neighborhood (an area where 80 percent of the population lives in public housing and where the average income for a family of four hovers around $14,000), the farm has become a training ground for dozens of local teenagers who grow dozens of crops in a foot-and-a-half of compost and soil mounded on top of the asphalt. (The compost/soil mix was originally supplied courtesy of the Bronx Zoo, which explains its fertility.) In this 2¾-acre space flourishes a diverse array of vegetables, everything from Mexican specialties such as pepiche and papalo to arugula, tomatoes, corn, and eggplants. Enough produce is grown to supply a farmers' market, six local restaurants, and a forty-member Community Shared Agriculture program. In 2008, the farm generated roughly $35,000 in sales. The value to the teen participants, who are paid for their work and learn job skills, is, of course, something that can't be quantified in dollars alone. "We're growing citizens not farmers," says Ian Marvy, cofounder and executive director of Added Value, "teaching new knowledge, new skills and, hopefully, a desire to make change in the world." He tells me of the young woman who, after participating in the farm project, tattooed the words "food justice" on her back.

While the money side of the equation—the financial benefits of urban farm projects like Red Hook—might seem like small potatoes, it all comes down to a question of how one quantifies value.

An empty lot serving as little more than a magnet for garbage, or a disintegrating ball field growing weeds through its cracked surface, contributes precisely zilch to a community and, more likely, diminishes it. Transforming such a place to productive purpose may yield relatively little in the way of financial return but much in the way of community benefits. Consider what one youth intern had to say at the groundbreaking ceremony for an urban farm project in San Francisco, in the summer of 1995: "We're not selling drugs like we used to, we're not dead like we're supposed to be and we're not in jail like we should be." No price tag can capture that.

What exactly is vacant land empty of? We could say buildings, but that isn't quite right because parks and waterfronts and a whole host of other urban places may be without buildings and still never be characterized as vacant. No, what's missing is care, intention, and attention. Vacant land violates our notions of purpose and plan, and the term itself is a kind of shorthand that carries our offended sensibilities, our response to neglect. But if we repeat and remember—vacant land is . . . *land*—the lens through which we peer at it can change, and the view with it.

Megan Horst of the University of Washington, College of Architecture and Urban Planning, effected precisely this perceptual shift in her 2008 report *Growing Green: An Inventory of Public Lands Suitable for Community Gardening in Seattle, Washington.* In an effort to provide an inventory for Seattle's Department of Neighborhoods, she assessed publicly owned land in the city in terms of its potential for community gardens, called P-Patches. In other words, she added a potential layer of care and intention to the city's vacant, excess, and unused parcels of land and found forty-five sites comprising more than 12 acres to be suitable for urban agriculture. If this inventory were indeed tapped, it would increase Seattle's existing P-Patch inventory—seventy-two gardens on 23 acres of land—by roughly half again. Considering that the waiting list for P-Patch plots in 2008 stretched to 1,500 people, clearly there's more than enough demand, more than enough people ready and willing to add their own layers of attention and intention.

A number of cities have taken the tentative first steps of identifying the potential that lurks in their vacant land resources (note the perceptual inversion: the vacant land is an asset not a problem). The Cuyahoga County Planning Commission, for example, has compiled a vacant land inventory as part of an investigation into land that would be suitable for urban agriculture in Cleveland. This approach is light years away from the response that city planners gave Moura Quayle, a professor at the University of British Columbia, when she did a survey for her groundbreaking 1986 *Report on Community Gardening in Canada*. Planners were asked why there were no community gardens in their jurisdictions, and several suggested lack of suitable land as a reason.

Clearly, there's a disconnect. There's no shortage of available land: the Brookings Institution, based in Washington, D.C., for example, surveyed seventy U.S. cities and published a report in 2000 called *Vacant Land in Cities: An Urban Resource*. The study revealed that, in each of the surveyed cities, there was an average of 12,000 acres of vacant or abandoned properties, or 15 percent of the total land area. The shortage isn't land; it's structural mechanisms and incentives that would kick-start programs aimed at transforming neglect into productivity.

The province of British Columbia provides one example of what that encouragement might look like. Legislation gives property owners a tax break if they convert empty lots into parks or public garden plots. Vancouver developer Prima Properties Ltd. took advantage of this program, saving $345,000 in annual property

Dig That Compost

VACANT-LOT GARDENING presents special challenges, not only in terms of negotiating access and ownership but also in terms of soil quality. Years of neglect, if not outright abuse, can leave urban soils desperately in need of improvement. As Chicago's City Farm and Brooklyn's Red Hook Community Farm have proven, though, compost can work wonders. Much in the same way that these vacant-lot gardening projects turned neglect into productivity, compost likewise turns waste into resource.

On a backyard scale, setting up some kind of compost system—whether an unenclosed heap (for yard waste only; adding food scraps will attract critters) or a more secure bin (to which food scraps can be added)—is a relatively straightforward proposition. There are numerous bins on the market, from simple one-bin units to deluxe models with three chambers, which make it easy to turn materials and store compost in various stages of "done-ness." I've experimented with many different commercial bins and my current favorite, by a long shot, is a barrel composter given to me by my brother. It couldn't be better for city applications: completely enclosed, and thus rodent-proof, it rests off the ground on a pivot, and it's very easy to turn the barrel, which mixes the materials thoroughly and speeds up decomposition. The only downside is that such barrel composters tend to be expensive. But they're worth their weight in gold because they're impervious to the rats and raccoons that can severely test the mettle of even the most committed urban compost enthusiast.

If a barrel is beyond your budget and you've gone with a more conventional unit that rests on the ground, you might want to consider rat-proofing your bin, particularly if you live in an area with a rodent problem. Don't believe the manufacturer's hype when they say their plastic (even thick, heavy plastic) bin will keep out rats. I've had rats chew through supposedly rat-proof plastic compost bins like they were made of paper, and, of course, rats can easily tunnel underneath any unprotected bin resting directly on the ground. Thus, reinforcements are in order. Line the bottom and sides of the bin with wire mesh or hardware cloth to foil these crafty creatures.

Composting your food waste is possible even if you live in an apartment and a regular bin is not an option. You can produce excellent compost for food plants in containers on your balcony, for example, using a vermicomposter. "Vermi" means worms and yes, these little wrigglers do the decomposition work for you. Vermicomposters (I've heard them called "worm farms" and I like the productive suggestiveness of this name) are commercially available and basically consist of a container that houses both the bedding (shredded newspaper, sawdust, dead leaves) and the worms. But be forewarned: you need to be vigilant about chopping up food scraps and careful not to overload the bin. Friends of mine plopped their Halloween pumpkin, the whole thing at once, into the bin, and suffered through an infestation of bugs and flies. Many cities offer subsidized compost bins and vermicomposters to residents, so be sure to check with city hall before plunking down money for a commercial bin.

tax, when it created a 100-plot vegetable garden on the site of an old gas station in the city's west end (after first replacing the soil to a depth of 6 meters, due to contamination). The developer had plans to build a condominium tower, but the economic downturn delayed construction. In went the Davie Village Community Garden, and the plots immediately filled, with a waiting list of 150 people on hold. A nonprofit organization, the Vancouver Public Space Network, supervises the project, thus relieving the city of any administrative drain on resources. Sounds like a winning proposition all round. What the city gets for that reduced tax rate is an urban eyesore turned into growing space, a place where more than 100 people exercise care and raise food. What the developer gets, beyond the tax break, is lots of community goodwill and lots of free labor in terms of maintaining the site. What everyone gets is a temporary problem turned into a temporary resource.

Other cities have come up with more permanent solutions. In 1996, a unique public sector organization in Chicago, called NeighborSpace, was created through a partnership between the Department of Planning and Development, the Chicago Parks District, and the Cook County Forest Preserve District. NeighborSpace, as its name suggests, acquires land for the purposes of open-space projects in the city; once the land is purchased it is deeded to community organizations that carry out and manage the growing projects. Through this mechanism, more than sixty new community gardens have been created in Chicago, many of them growing on what was once tax-delinquent land. One of the crucial features that allows this program to work is that NeighborSpace, through the volume of land it acquires, is able to provide group insurance to the gardens, something that would be impossible for the gardeners to do on their own.

There's the rub—liability issues often trump creative solutions, especially in relation to vacant land. In our lawsuit-embracing culture, in which so many responsibility questions are resolved through legal proceedings, it's inevitable that liability concerns often cut creativity off at the knees. And one of the biggest liability concerns of vacant land is toxic contamination. Abandoned industrial sites present all manner of hazards, including toxic chemicals such as petroleum and oil, lead, other heavy metals, volatile organic compounds, pesticides, and polycyclic aromatic hydrocarbons. The toxic chemicals range from the obvious and known (those reported by the company) to the hidden (those unknown or forgotten, which may, for example, be leaking from underground storage tanks). Even vacant residential properties may be contaminated—demolished houses can leave a legacy of lead from old paint, the soil burdened with unsafe levels of this heavy metal that doesn't biodegrade or decay.

The pattern of development in North American cities is such that pollution and poverty go hand in hand. It's no surprise that when the Toronto-based organization PollutionWatch looked at the connection between low-income areas and industrial emissions, they found that a high percentage of Toronto's poorest residents live close to industries that legally release the highest levels of toxic chemicals and pollutants into the air. And it is these low-income, industrial areas of North American cities that tend to accumulate abandoned land. (When was the last time you saw a vacant lot in the tonier part of town?) Thus, a double whammy—those places where the need for food is greatest and where the land resources exist that could be used to at least partially meet that need are also the places where land (and air) is most contaminated.

Mary Seton Corboy didn't let that stop her. Back in the late 1990s, she and Tom Sereduk, both former chefs, realized that the restaurants of Philadelphia represented a ready market for fresh vegetables: "It seemed to us that the shortest distance between supply and demand must have some real savings to it." They both lived in Philadelphia and thought that maybe they could grow food commercially on some of the city's vacant land. The site they chose for their farm, Greensgrow, had been home to Boyles Galvanizing, a steel plant. The buildings had been demolished in 1988 and the land, contaminated with arsenic, zinc, and lead, had been cleaned up (remediated) by the U.S. Environmental Protection Agency. It sat empty for eight years. There was no water, electrical, or gas service to the lot and it was surrounded by a chain-link fence. In other words, the site shouted "keep out." On the other hand, it was also cheap and available. Corboy and Sereduk took the plunge, investing thousands in the construction of a hydroponic growing system. In their first year of operation, 1998, they earned approximately $18,000 selling gourmet lettuce (450 pounds a week) to fifteen high-end restaurants. In 1999, their earnings increased to $32,000 and they branched out in 2000, building a large four-season greenhouse and opening a nursery selling seedlings they raised in the greenhouse. On 4,500 square feet of raised beds, they added tomatoes, potatoes, and herbs to their production and opened a farm stand on the site to sell their produce to locals in the economically disadvantaged area, the Port Richmond section of north Philadelphia.

In stark contrast to the "keep out, no trespassing" message the site had broadcast during its former existence as a contaminated brownfield, Greensgrow now exists as a decidedly social place, a community hub. (It helps that there's a bus stop across the street from the farm.) Visitors are encouraged to wander through the farm, and tours are offered to groups. Flowers now grace the chain-link fence. "For the first few years we were unsure of whether we were the animals inside the urban zoo or we were watching the urban zoo," says Corboy. "When we decided to start growing flowers the fence came down. Not literally but metaphorically. People wandered in and stayed to ask us about the food we were growing.

Never in our early years did we envision Greensgrow as a community hub. Now it's hard to believe it hasn't always been this way."

Not only do people come to the farm stand, but the farm stand goes to the people: when the director of a local seniors' center mentioned that some senior residents weren't mobile enough to come to the market, Greensgrow decided to add a new service, wheeling a cart of produce directly to the seniors.

Such community connections extend beyond the local neighborhood as well. Greensgrow has been involved in forming the Neighborhood Urban Agriculture Coalition (NUAC), whose vision is to establish a network of small urban farms in low-income communities and not only sell the produce from these urban farms but also distribute the products of rural farm members of the NUAC cooperative. As Corboy puts it, "The urban farmer becomes, in essence, the neighborhood grocer of years gone by. We are the liaison between the urban consumer and the rural producer—a role that the modern food system has neglected to fill and so people lost touch with food."

Greensgrow has also initiated the Center for Urban Agriculture, assisting individuals and groups who are interested in starting their own projects, sharing the wisdom they've learned through a decade of trial and error. With self-deprecating humor, Corboy doesn't hold herself up as a guru but rather as someone with a couple of battle-scar notches on her belt: "Farming is a vocation not a vacation, and farming in someone else's backyard is not going to necessarily win you friends. It takes time, money, physical labor under very harsh conditions, sweat, tears, and a vocabulary list of insurances that breaks your heart and wallet. Think first, dive later."

On an acre of industrial brownfield once considered virtually unusable, Greensgrow has made a successful and community-minded something out of nothing. Corboy is clearly proud of the

87

fact that the farm has turned waste into resource: "Almost everything at Greensgrow has been begged, borrowed, or trash picked,"
she says, adding that "it is one of the ironies of urban agricultural
development that these former industrial sites are in fact some of
the best choices for locating a new urban agricultural business."
They are readily available and they are often located in low-
income neighborhoods where access to fresh food is hard to come
by, thus ensuring a market for the farm's produce and providing a
valuable social service. While there is no doubt that formerly contaminated land presents specific challenges to the growing of food,
projects like Greensgrow prove that the problems can be overcome.
As Corboy reminds us, "Abandoned land is only abandoned if we
choose to leave it that way."

History provides another reminder. In the late nineteenth and
early twentieth centuries, North American cities turned their
attention to vacant lots, choosing *not* to leave them that way.
One of the earliest food-growing organizations, the Committee for the Cultivation of Vacant Lots, was established in Boston
in 1895. This charity leased 60 acres of farmland near Franklin
Park to grow food for the poor. A few years later, in 1898, Philadelphia sponsored a vacant lot program. The purpose of such
programs was three-fold: to improve the appearance of cities, to
provide employment for the growing number of people migrating
from rural to urban areas, and to produce food for the urban poor.
Although the emphasis shifted according to the priorities of the
time, the vacant lot movement continued for decades and found
expression in many urban centers. In Canada, the City Improvement League of Montreal, founded in 1909, turned vacant lots
into children's gardens. By 1916, the Toronto Vacant Lots Cultivation Association, formed in 1914, was gardening 2,060 lots; in
the same year, Montreal had 5,000, their popularity so great that

officials noted that they could have filled three times as many lots with gardens. By 1917, the smaller Ontario community of Guelph had 1,600 vacant lots planted mainly with potatoes.

Members of Calgary's Vacant Lots Garden Club, active from 1914 to the 1950s, paid $1 per year for membership and tended more than 3,000 plots. (Three of those sites are still in existence as community gardens and have been designated as municipal historic resources.) During World War I, the Ottawa Horticultural Society formed a Vacant Lot Association and, during the Depression, it assisted in the Relief Gardens for the Unemployed initiative. As happened with Victory Gardens, however, the enthusiasm for vacant-lot gardening was not sustained beyond times of crisis. As Moura Quayle explains in a 1989 essay in *Landscape Architecture Review*, "the movement's energy began to dwindle as people felt more affluent and less reliant on homegrown food to supplement their diet."

Yet also like Victory Gardens, the promotion of vacant-lot gardening was at one time undertaken at the highest levels. In 1917, Canada's dominion horticulturist, W.T. Macoun, inaugurated a vacant-lot gardening poetry contest to spread interest in the campaign. The first-prize winner that year was Henrietta Wood. While history might be less than kind to some of her lines ("Here grow my cabbages, dew-pearled at dawn"), perhaps history could take note of another: "Behold my Vacant Lot, vacant no more."

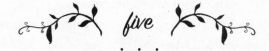

RETHINKING CONVENTION
FINDING SOIL AND SITES

I'M AN IMPATIENT gardener, and lazy to boot. As deadly as this combination might sound—deadly to plants, that is—it has led me to some surprisingly productive shortcuts. My tomato farm, for example. Given that my backyard is full to bursting with trees and getting shadier by the day, I figured that tomatoes were not an option in the garden proper. And I'd already filled the patio with pots growing herbs, salad greens, and scarlet runner beans trained up the wall with string. I was happily resigned to growing tomatoes in my community garden plot about a mile away, and supplementing my own tomatoes with market purchases.

But then I looked up, and that's when my prospects of backyard tomato production also started looking up. Attached to the back of my house is a small mudroom where I keep gardening tools, shoes, snow shovels, folding chairs, and a whole host of outdoor necessities. The room has a door to the backyard, is about 8 feet tall, and is topped with a gently sloping roof. Crucially, for tomatoes, it's a sun-baked spot, easily accessed by simply setting up a stepladder. And so I decided to create the world's lowest-maintenance rooftop tomato mini-farm.

No engineers were required to test the weight-bearing capacity of the roof through complex calculations; no waterproof membranes had to be installed by contractors trained in construction; no permits were needed from the city, nor advice from experts. I simply lugged four bags of topsoil up the ladder and plunked each one down on the hot black shingles. Using a kitchen knife, I sliced two x's in the top of each bag (careful not to cut through the bottom of the bag) and planted a tomato seedling in each slit. Then I surrounded each plant with a wire tomato cage and *voila*, I had a decidedly perky-looking tomato plantation.

Like soldiers lined up in a row, ready for anything, my tomato plants weathered storms—the cages listed only slightly in the wind—and proved too far out of reach for the raccoons and squirrels. I watered them regularly with manure tea and gave them a fertilizer boost a couple of times over the summer.

The tomatoes started forming fruit quite early in the growing season: tiny White Currants, Green Zebras, Black Prince. It was a colorful kaleidoscope up there, my little sky garden.

WHAT DO YOU do when you've either run out of gardening space or don't have much to begin with? Land is a luxury in most big cities, and many of us make do with little of it. But tucked away in hidden corners—and sometimes staring us in the face—are places of possibility, areas that just require some ingenuity to reach their growing potential. I've seen all kinds of gardens in the unlikeliest of places, and each one inspires. My recent favorite is the one created by the crafty cyclist who turned the back end of her bike into a moveable feast: attached to a small carrying platform on the fender was an herb farm, basil and thyme poking out of the soil contained in a tiny wooden box. The herbs looked very healthy indeed. I suspect that this person was not a speed cyclist, since wind shear would surely do damage. Instead, I imagine this cyclist meandering through city streets at a slow pace, the scent of basil perfuming the air behind her. Another bike-themed garden I admired was the old bicycle helmet turned into the world's smallest container garden. And then there was the sun hat, turned into the world's second smallest container garden, a tomato poking up from the brim . . . In other words, ingenuity (and no fear of being laughed at) is what's required of the gardener who lacks traditional growing space.

Ismael Hautecoeur of Montreal is expert at ferreting out the possible places that surround us. A landscape architect and philosopher by training ("so I know how to argue and how to make things look beautiful"), he's used to casting a critical eye on urban form, but the growing spaces he's had a hand in cultivating are not the high-end yards of those who can afford professional services. Rather, he focuses on the vernacular, and in Montreal that means balconies and impossibly winding iron staircases twisting from the ground up. Hautecoeur rigs a system of string supports to the balconies and railings of buildings to create instant—and small space—gardens in what would otherwise be open air. He plants beans that grow up the strings and produce a green, edible wall. "When I sit on the porch having a beer, people ask me, 'What are you doing?' And I tell them, 'I'm watching the bean race.'"

Hautecoeur likes to remind budding urban gardeners that "you don't need high-tech stuff. Everything is there—you just have to put it together." Slightly more elaborate but equally easy to create using simple materials is his "staircase lettuce" plantation. It consists of open tubing filled with soil and wound around the fire escape. "If there's a fire, you harvest quickly," he advises.

93

The balcony gardeners of Toronto's St. James Town pride themselves in repurposing and recycling found objects as containers for their inventive projects. This large city block of high-rise apartment buildings is home to more than 30,000 people—one of the highest densities in the country—and many of the residents are recent immigrants. Nandiny Pirapakaran and Lara Lucretia run a balcony gardening project at the neighborhood social service agency, Growing Together, a program of The Hincks-Dellcrest Centre. "In my country," says Nandiny, a Tamil originally from Sri Lanka, "a lot of people grow plants in the ground. But when people come here, to apartments, they don't have gardens. We show them how they can grow their own food on the balcony, so they won't feel frustrated without gardening space." Every year since 2003, approximately fifty families have signed up for the project. In mid-February, they start seedlings in a children's greenhouse at Allan Gardens, a local park. Nandiny and Lara conduct workshops on Saturdays, engaging kids in gardening activities designed for fun but often disguising useful lessons. For the Space Invaders activity, one pot is planted with just one radish seed and other pots are planted with five, ten, and twenty seeds—when it comes time to harvest, kids see firsthand that crowded plants don't yield much, a lesson they can take home to their own balcony plots. For the Garbage Garden, leftovers from afternoon snacks become fodder for growing experiments. When the kids finish an orange or an avocado, they plant the seeds and watch them grow in the greenhouse, eventually taking the plants home. St. James Town balconies thus house probably the highest density of orange trees in all of Toronto.

While Nandiny and Lara keep statistics on balcony gardeners who have signed up with the project at Growing Together, they don't know how many others of St. James Town's 30,000 residents

are growing food on their balconies. However, they do keep photo-
graphs of the balcony gardens they've visited. As we click through
the digital images together, they highlight one interesting growing method after another: the Cuban woman who hangs tomato
plants *upside down* from the balcony ceiling, a sponge keeping the
soil from spilling out of the inverted pot; the cabbage leaves that
sprout from a discarded cabbage core planted in a container; the
bottom of a leek likewise planted in a small pot and now producing
new leaves; the bitter melon vine twisting up strings hung along
the balcony; the potatoes grown in a bushel basket lined with a
garbage bag into which small holes have been poked; the pear tree
that winters indoors . . .

"Some people just have two plants, some have twenty-two,"
says Lara, "but for people who don't have green space on the
ground, this is a great way to make use of high-density urban
space." It's also a great way to make use of materials that would
otherwise go to the landfill. Lara and Nandiny are planning to
extend the project to include balcony composting, since there is
currently no organic waste collection from high-rise apartment
buildings in Toronto. A volunteer is collecting used pickle buckets
from a local submarine sandwich shop, which will eventually be
turned into small compost bins. "We're constantly demonstrating
that it's possible to do container gardening without purchasing
fancy supplies," Lara and Nandiny write on the Toronto Balconies
Bloom website. "There's a lot you can do by reusing materials at
hand."

Even something as low-tech as a clothesline can be enlisted in
the food-growing effort. As well as in the drink-growing effort.
Ben Granger, an owner of Bierkraft in Brooklyn, grows a dozen
different varieties of hop vines in his tiny backyard, a clothesline
and pullies and trellises providing the support. As he puts it: "I'm

95

mimicking the way the city grew. It grew up not out." In 2009, he grew enough hops for a 10-gallon batch of beer.

This is a somewhat more formalized system than what ended up happening to my neighbor at my old house: a zucchini vine got away from his eternal vigilance (this was a gardener who spent most of his days tending his intensive backyard farm—someone who wrapped his fig tree in insulation and buried it each fall, after harvesting buckets of figs before the squirrels ate them) and twined its way up the telephone pole and then vertically along the wires. All of the neighbors in our cramped little community watched with interest—and some concern for the workings of our phone lines—as the weight of the vegetables dragged the wire lower and lower . . .

With a bit more planning, the dangling technique can be quite effective. I'm thinking of growing potatoes in sacks hanging from the window. At ReVision Urban Farm in Boston, the south-facing balconies of the social housing project for homeless young women and their children have been turned into "bioshelters"—big greenhouse-style hydroponic systems—for residents to grow vegetables in. (And, even more impressive, to raise tilapia fish in, as part of an aquaculture project.)

Also tapping into the untapped potential of walls is the Urban Farming Food Chain in Los Angeles, a project established by the international nonprofit organization Urban Farming, in partnership with local "host" groups. Using a commercially available system developed by Green Living Technologies, the groups grow fresh produce—fruits and vegetables—on an assortment of walls throughout the city. They're currently nurturing more than 750 square feet of edible vertical landscapes on buildings, concrete walls, and parking lot walls. Along with food for humans (plants such as bell peppers, tomatillos, spinach, and leeks), these green walls offer habitat for pollinating insects. Of course, people also enjoy the beauty and the comforting, cooling effects that result from vegetative cover. (Note that humans aren't the only ones who can be fed by green walls. Paignton Zoo in England has installed a vertical farm—growing plants in trays of water moving on a conveyor belt—that provides a supply of lettuce and other edibles for the zoo's animals.) Green Living Technologies has also partnered with the Vancouver nonprofit Environmental Youth Alliance to install a vertical food-growing wall in Blood Alley—the first edible wall in Vancouver, and possibly in Canada.

If walls represent a distinctly urban frontier of food production, green roofs aren't far behind in the pushing-the-envelope department. The common refrain—there just isn't enough room in cities to grow food—gets turned on its head when you re-frame the definition of "room." When conventional land is in short supply, we've got rooftop space in abundance. A 1998 estimate published in *Environmental Building News* magazine calculated that the 4.8 million commercial buildings in the United States have approximately 1,400 square miles of rooftop space, the majority of it low-slope. This represents an area larger than the state of Rhode Island. Of course, not all of those roofs are structurally designed to support the added weight of soil that food growing would require, and not all of them are accessible, but it's an evocative number nevertheless and it suggests the question: just how many of those 1,400 square miles could be used to grow food?

My own little low-tech rooftop experiment was a revelation, and there are plenty of people exploring the potential of rooftop food production on a much larger scale. Toronto architect Monica Kuhn, an early promoter of green roofs in Canada, grows an extensive vegetable garden in containers on the flat roof of her home (a home that, appropriately enough, is in an area of Toronto called

97

Edible Plants to Attract Beneficial Insects

THE VAST majority of insects that visit gardens are actually beneficial. They do important pollination work, provide food for birds, eat other pests that can harm plants, and much more. The following edible (for humans) plants are especially good for attracting beneficial insects.

- > coriander/cilantro
- > fennel
- > lavender
- > lemon balm
- > mint

- > calendula
- > dill
- > chervil
- > rosemary
- > thyme

....

Cabbagetown, in reference to the market gardens that once flourished there).

While the expense of retrofitting an existing single-dwelling home to bear the added weight might be out of reach for many (1 cubic foot of soil, when saturated with water, weighs approximately 100 pounds), some forward-thinking developers are taking that carrying capacity into consideration and building it right into their plans. A recent Vancouver condominium project includes raised beds on the rooftop. Residents can purchase a plot, much as they would a parking space. (The plots that haven't yet been sold are gardened by Ward Teulon of City Farm Boy, who grows garlic and carrots in these sky-high raised beds—"Rooftops are a good spot to grow carrots," he says. "Carrot flies can't get up there.") Likewise, the Burnside Rocket building in Portland has a 1,000-square-foot garden on its roof. In addition to six raised beds, there are less conventional plots: dozens of kids' wading pools have been turned into planters. Food grown on the rooftop supplies a wine bar restaurant on the top floor of the building, Nobel Rot.

If condo rooftops call out for domestic vegetable production, supermarket roofs represent their retail equivalent. Sky Vegetables, a Berkeley, California, company, hopes to install food-growing systems on supermarket rooftops—taking the idea of local food to literally new heights—though they'll no doubt need to find structures more solid than the flimsily constructed box stores proliferating throughout North America.

Hotels and restaurants are also obvious candidates for rooftop food production. The chefs who work at the largest hotel kitchen in Canada, the Fairmont Royal York in Toronto, make the daily trek up to the roof garden to pick heritage tomatoes, eggplants, alpine strawberries, edible flowers, red romaine lettuce, and more than sixty varieties of herbs. (The bartender, in particular, appreciates the mint.) Before then-executive chef George McNeill started the garden in 1998, the roof wasn't used for anything. Now, says chef David Garcelon, the cooks who make their way through the humming mechanical room and out onto the roof "get a little more connected with where their food comes from." They also visit the bees. In 2008, the hotel added three hives to the garden (and renamed a few of the hotel's special rooms the V.I.Bee Suite, the Royal Sweet, and the Honey Moon Suite). In the first season, the hives produced 380 pounds of honey. "We use a lot more honey in our cooking now," says Garcelon, noting with pride that their honey recently won second prize in the Amber Liquid Honey category and third in the Dark Amber category at the Royal Winter Fair. The Toronto Beekeepers Co-operative helps with the hives, and in 2009 another three hives were added. Garcelon is also proud of another pet project of his up on the roof: three grape vines, which he calls "the world's smallest vineyard." He admits that the vines take a lot of work (he wraps them in burlap for the winter) and that from the grapes he harvested in 2008, he could probably make a grand total of two glasses of wine, but even so, there's something exciting about a vineyard growing fourteen stories up in the air.

Imagine going out to dinner at a restaurant and knowing that some of the food on your plate was grown above your head. At Chicago's Uncommon Ground—a restaurant that should perhaps be called Uncommon Roof instead—customers dine on food produced on the first certified organic roof farm in the U.S. After reinforcing the roof to handle 6 tons of soil, a 2,500-square-foot fruit and vegetable garden was planted 30 feet above the street. Four beehives produce honey (40 pounds were harvested in 2008). It's not just the diners who benefit from this fresh food—the restaurant also conducts garden workshops with local schools.

Making connections between rooftop food production and the neighboring community is even more explicit at Vancouver's downtown YWCA administration offices. Their garden is five floors up, and the organic harvest—560 kilograms in 2009—goes to the YWCA's Crabtree Corner community kitchen, where it is used in meals for women and kids of the Downtown Eastside neighborhood, one of the neediest communities in the country. Collingwood Neighbourhood House, also in Vancouver, uses the food from its rooftop garden in meal programs for seniors, families in need, and homeless people. Adding to the social benefits of the project is the drop-in gardening party they host every week in the summer.

One of the longest-running rooftop vegetable gardens in Canada (aside from container gardens on roof decks of private homes, that is) had an unusual beginning. Professor Tom Hutchinson of Trent University in Peterborough, Ontario, initially started the planting on the roof of the Environmental Studies building as part of his research, which monitors the effects of air pollution on vegetable crops. He didn't consider himself a rooftop pioneer; rather, he was just trying to ensure that his research wouldn't be eaten by deer. But his research is now eaten by students—with his permission. The vegetables, including many heirloom varieties, herbs, and edible flowers, are used in the campus' student-run, cooperative restaurant, the Seasoned Spoon Café.

The agricultural use of urban rooftops is still a long way from becoming something even approaching common. I suspect that one of the best ways to ensure that it does so is to involve kids and students, much the way that Uncommon Ground and the Seasoned Spoon Café have. Surely the kids at the Université du Québec à Montréal's day care, who eat food grown on the UQAM design building's rooftop terrace, or the teenagers who plant, harvest, and eat the vegetables from the green roof at Chicago's Gary Comer Youth Center, will grow up with a decidedly expanded notion of urban possibility. Perhaps, when they look up, they'll see farms and food instead of empty space.

Setting our sights closer to the ground also reveals unlikely places full of possibility. My friend Doug has a flourishing tall-grass prairie garden in his front yard and a wet-meadow planting on his boulevard, but he wanted to grow heirloom vegetables as well. So, in a narrow strip of land between his driveway and his neighbor's lawn, he planted tomatoes, zucchini, peas, and peppers, and has managed to harvest a surprising amount of food (including 31 pounds of tomatoes in 2009)—all from an area just 4 feet wide by about 15 feet long. One thing often leads to another. Doug has now set his sights on the driveway itself. Since he doesn't own

> City Bees

MICHAEL THOMPSON takes the subway to visit his beehives. A cofounder of the Chicago Honey Co-op, he helps take care of eight hives on three different rooftops for the city of Chicago (including two hives on the roof of city hall) and he manages the co-op's bee farm—anywhere from 60 to 100 hives lined up on an ex-parking lot in the city's west end. An old hand at urban apiculture (he's been teaching beekeeping for forty years), Thompson is both an enthusiastic *and* realistic advocate: "It's incredibly hard work," he cautions, "as hard as any kind of farming—backbreaking, hot, sweaty work, and we love it!"

People are often surprised to hear that the urban environment can be more conducive to beekeeping than rural areas. "Cities have abundant quantity and diversity of nectar sources—clovers, all the trees . . . ," says Thompson. What cities likewise have in abundance are spaces ideal for beehives: rooftops, railway rights of way, empty lots, parkland. And yes, cities also have an abundance of people who are afraid of bees. "A lot of people mistake honeybees for yellow jacket wasps and hornets. But honeybees are very gentle," says Thompson. "You have to kick a hive to get in trouble."

Some cities have outright bans on beehives; others have restrictions specifying the distance hives must be kept from property lines or buildings, and still others have gone from bee bans to bee promotion. Vancouver, for example, removed its prohibition against urban apiaries and now allows small-scale backyard beekeeping; the Vancouver Convention Centre has 60,000 bees on its green roof. (Honeybees are not the only bees finding favor in Vancouver—in 2008, the Environmental Youth Alliance began distributing mason-bee condos to participating homeowners and installing the bee condos in parks and public spaces. The goal is to increase the bee population and mitigate the decline of these crucial pollinators.)

As they forage for nectar, honeybees move pollen, thus contributing to more productive harvests in food gardens. While managing a hive might be more work than many of us want to take on, let's hope that other adventurous urban farmers feel inspired to give it a try. Michael Thompson offers the following suggestions for novice urban beekeepers: "Talk to the neighbors before any investment. Make sure they are in agreement with your hobby. Take a class and read some books on the subject. Make friends with an existing beekeeper—someone you can call with your many questions."

And if your municipality has a no-hive rule, consider the advice provided by Kerry Banks, back in the first issue of *City Farmer Newspaper* in 1978: "keep your hedges high, your head low and your neighbour's honey jar well-filled."

a car, he's thinking of tearing up the asphalt and planting a "hive-way," for the bees that pollinate his crops.

If that's too drastic, there are other, less permanent ways to eke space out of the asphalt and concrete that cities have in abundance. On the unused parking lot in the west end of Chicago where the Chicago Honey Co-op keeps its hives, the group has planted sweet potatoes and squash in mounds of compost that are layered on top of the concrete. On a parking lot at the Brick Works, a Toronto park, the nonprofit group Evergreen one year added small mounds of soil and planted vegetables in little hillocks. It was about as make-do-with-what-you've-got as you can get. Watering had to be done carefully, to avoid erosion, but other than that it was a very basic, low-tech setup.

Containers, of course, provide a bit more structure and have the added advantage of being compact and moveable. Like my neighbor down the street, gardeners in tight spaces have always found ingenious ways to repurpose just about anything—old leaky rubber boots, olive oil tins, wine barrels, garbage cans, cat trays—into growing space. Making the job easier are some recent innovations in container design. One of the trickier challenges of container growing is that the pots dry out very quickly, necessitating daily vigilance and maintenance. Ismael Hautecoeur, working with Alternatives, an international development NGO, has developed lightweight self-watering tubs that make container growing, particularly on rooftops, much simpler. (A guide available at rooftopgardens.ca explains how to build your own. Another source, urbanorganicgardener.com, has a detailed description of how to make a self-watering container.)

My favorite example of container innovation, though, is a combo composter/planter made by Marco Pagliarulo for his fifth-floor balcony in a Toronto high-rise. I met Marco while judging a container garden contest at a farmers' market, and he won the prize. But if he hadn't helpfully added a sign to his container saying "Composter," it's possible that the other judges and I wouldn't have noticed the container's double purpose, so artfully disguised was the compost function. A lidded container—a simple white plastic food container, the kind that restaurants buy bulk food in—was nestled in an attractive planter. This smaller lidded container was the compost bin, with a cover for the food wastes, small holes poked in the sides for drainage and in the lid for air, and the bottom removed. Soil was packed at the bottom of the planter and around the smaller container, and planted with tomatoes, basil, parsley, and dill. The sprawling plants hid the lid. A small trapdoor cut out at the bottom of the planter allowed for easy access to the compost, which Marco regularly stirred. The plants and soil absorbed any excess moisture seeping out of the compost. With this simple, homemade arrangement, Marco was able to recycle all of his vegetable scraps *and* harvest a container's worth of food that was nourished by last month's dinner. "It looks quite nice and it doesn't smell," says Marco of his inventive combo.

The repurposing of materials into structures to use in small places—cultivation bags, cultivation racks, cultivation ladders, umbrellas, antennae—is not limited to above-ground expression. In one of the more unlikely re-uses, Winnipeg teacher Dave Taylor, in the early 2000s, asked the Winnipeg Police Department and the local RCMP detachment for hydroponic growing equipment confiscated from illegal marijuana operations. Permission granted, he set up a different kind of grow op: Winnipeg's first hydroponic urban greenhouse. Like illegal grow ops, this one was hidden— it was underground, in the lower area of a downtown building owned by the Canadian National Railway. With trains rumbling overhead, this hydroponic operation was an educational facility where unemployed, at-risk youth gained horticultural experience and practical work experience. The produce, all basil, was sold to restaurants. "Some people said we were teaching bad habits," says Taylor, acknowledging that hydroponic growing skills could be transferred to illegal crops, "but what they were learning was incredible"—the tricky skills needed to control pests organically in a greenhouse, for example. Taylor hoped to expand the project to other schools and to aboriginal communities in the province of Manitoba, but federal funding for the project was cut off in 2005.

Along with hidden places, there are obvious but rarely used areas that could be used for food production. Consider, for example, the possibilities of floating farms on urban waterways. Manhattan had one on the Hudson River in 2007. Called the Science Barge, this 135-foot-long boat was rigged up as a hydroponic greenhouse, powered by solar and wind energy and biofuels, to grow tomatoes, cucumbers, peppers, lettuce, squash, and herbs. If this sounds like a wacky, one-off project, British Waterways doesn't think so. They're considering using retired workboats as floating vegetable gardens along the hundreds of miles of canals for which they're responsible. They're also looking for areas of land bordering London's canals and rivers that could be used to grow food.

Others have floated ideas that are even more of a stretch. Dickson Despommier, a professor at Columbia University, has explored and promoted the idea of hydroponic farms in cities through his Vertical Farm Project. Some proposals are fanciful (Vincent Callebaut Architectures' New York City skyscraper—a "bionic tower"—in the shape of a dragonfly wing), others are more modest (Rios Clementi Hale Studios' three-story "Incredible Edible House," made of stacked prefabricated containers). Who knows whether or not these ideas will go the way of earlier, Jetson-ish notions of what the urban future might hold, but one of their most enduring features is surely that they conceptualize buildings—and the cities these buildings are a part of—as living systems, productive rather than parasitic. Even though these are currently purely theoretical exercises, I for one feel heartened that architecture schools throughout North America seem to be bubbling with professors and students keen to design unique urban structures that push the food-growing envelope into imagination's stratosphere.

ROOFTOPS, UNDERGROUND BUNKERS, floating boats, highrises... These might seem to be very strange places for urban food production, but there's no doubt that they will come to be perceived as less odd over time. As more and more people start to garden these unconventional places, the gardens will be slowly absorbed into convention. We may even get to the point of wondering why it took us so long to see the potential of these, for now, unusual frontiers.

I predict that in the not too distant future, we will view front yards in this way. There are literally thousands and thousands of acres of front yards in North America devoted to a single crop: lawn grass. Decades of social messaging, at times propped up by legal coercion and always reinforced by corporate advertising, have convinced us that it is our duty and desire to cover the ground with green lawn carpeting that serves little functional purpose beyond confirming that we are compliant beings. Yes, lawn grass is a great platform for all kinds of activities, but when was the last time you saw a front-yard baseball game? The activity we most often carry out instead is lawn mowing.

All that grass—14 million hectares in the U.S. alone, an area the size of Iowa—requires more maintenance than the cornfields of Iowa. And so we spend billions ($9 billion in the U.S. in 1999;

107

$2 billion in Canada in 2006) keeping that monocultural carpet green, shorn, weed free, and bug free. Saturday mornings are devoted to noisy displays of care, pushing or riding the mower, and choreographed dances with the sprinkler, in an effort to stave off midsummer crisping of green to brown. Our lawn-care applications of pesticides and fertilizers likewise rival those used on the cornfields of Iowa. According to the U.S. Environmental Protection Agency (quoted in Paul Robbins's book *Lawn People*), 23 percent of the total 2,4-D applied in the U.S. in 1995 was used on lawns, along with 22 percent of glyphosate, 31 percent of chlorpyrifos, and 38 percent of dicamba.

Paul Robbins's book is actually one of the scarier (and more enlightening) tomes I've read in a while. A provocative ecological, economic, and social critique of the lawn in the urban context, the book argues that "the lawn has, since its inception, been proffered as an instrument both for maintaining growth in contemporary urban development and for creating a responsible domestic American citizen: a responsible, domestic kind of person. Rather than simply being an artifact of culture, then, the lawn is better understood as a vehicle for creating certain kinds of cultural subjects." Yikes. Lawns are us. Domesticated turfgrass subjects, our lives are disciplined by the dominant landscape form we've accepted as ruler—the lawn.

Aesthetics is one part of the rigid scaffolding that supports lawn dominance. Convention, endlessly repeated across North America, has taught us that a lawn is beautiful, weeds are ugly, and vegetables belong in the backyard. Yet surely there's room for more than one standardized notion of beauty. Garden writer Gayla Trail makes the revealing observation that the aesthetics of gardens are often most interesting when people stop worrying about the aesthetics. Surely variation and diversity in the front-yard department enriches the view. Surely we can celebrate the beauty of the lawn and still question the need for it everywhere . . .

Yet our tolerance for lawn dissent doesn't have a great track record. The rebels of the Midwestern states who first started planting tallgrass prairie gardens in their front yards were subjected to countless legal challenges and forced into court to defend their unconventional (but ecologically purposeful) landscaping choices. It has taken decades, but slowly the naturalized yard movement has reached a point of, if not widespread adoption, then at least sometimes celebrated, sometimes grudging, acceptance.

Lawn outlaws who dare to replace grass with food have also sometimes been met with legal sanction. When, in 2007, the Tall Gallery in suburban Calgary planted barley out front, they were slapped with a series of warnings and then a notice from the city saying that their "lawn" was infested with "objectionable" and "unsightly" weeds. According to Chris Turner, writing in the *Globe and Mail,* while the gallery's barley growers argued that they were creating a water-conserving, xeriscape garden, the city saw their efforts as an "agricultural pursuit . . . not within the ordinary meaning of a garden," and hence something that should not be allowed.

Historical examples of how the "ordinary meaning of a garden" has changed over the years are useful reminders that there's nothing at all ordinary about meaning. It is instead something collectively determined (forced, even) and it can just as determinedly be collectively changed in more sensible, more diverse, or simply more open-minded ways. When we look back through garden history at conventions that may have seemed so right at the time that they hardly even needed explanation or justification, we can find all kind of crazy coercions ripe for challenge. A popular 1956 gardening book, for example, *Complete Home Landscaping and Garden*

Guide, chides readers about "the use of flowers in the public area" of the front yard because of the "damage" they do to "the picture of your house as seen from the street." The author, Raymond Korbobo, acknowledges that, even so, many people "will insist on planting some there." Thus, he provides the suggestion that if one simply must indulge this "natural instinct" to grow flowers out front, that they be planted behind shrubs: "There they could not be seen easily from the street; yet the people living in the house could enjoy the view as they looked towards the flower beds." Yesterday's "hide the flowers" from public view is today's "hide the vegetables" from public view. Perhaps our construction of ordinary meaning could do with a little more deconstruction of what that ordinary meaning *means.*

HOW LONG WILL it take, I wonder, before front-yard vegetables become common in our communities? Of course, immigrants to North America have been doing it for years. In my city, you can easily locate yourself in an Italian, Portuguese, or Chinese neighborhood by taking note of the front-yard trellises supporting beans and squash vines or the rows of stakes propping up tomatoes. But you can equally track the gentrification of the neighborhood or the passing of a generation by the number of food gardens that revert back to lawn once the real estate agent's "sold" sign is taken down.

If food out front is still an anomaly in North American cities—too far from the lawn norm for acceptance by us turfgrass subjects—one promising approach offers a way to ease into aesthetic comfort. The edible landscape movement, pioneered and promoted by California garden writer Rosalind Creasy, proposes the inclusive idea that vegetable and fruit plants can, and should, be brought into the fold of ornamental garden design. Any doubters need only look at a colorful parade of rainbow chard to be

convinced that edibles can be beautiful. It's a simple but poten-
tially transforming idea. Creasy has written that when she planted
artichokes and herbs among the flowers in her front yard more
than thirty years ago, she was considered a "nut-case." Now her
edible landscape, with its potatoes, watermelons, cucumbers,
squash, and peppers interspersed with flowers, is renowned in the
garden world and featured in glossy magazine spreads.

I've noticed something weird—and, I think, highly revealing
of human foible—about gardens and plants in particular: when we
give something unfamiliar and convention-stretching a fancy or
catchy label, people are more likely to be okay with it. I saw this
first with my friend Doug's garden. He was getting all kinds of
sideways glances and rolled eyes about the tallgrass prairie plants
he'd installed in his front garden in a "lawn rules" suburban area
of Toronto. Some of his neighbors were not amused. So Doug
resorted to a sneaky trick. Off he went to the garden center to collect a slew of plant labels, those little markers that list the plant's
name and that people often put in the ground beside their plants
to remind them of what's where. Doug didn't worry one bit that
the names on the labels didn't match the native prairie plants in
his garden. What mattered was that the plants, although unfamiliar to the neighbors and thus a bit suspect, now had sanctioned
pedigree. The Latin on the labels proved it. And, sure enough, that
was enough reassurance for some of the neighbors. Doug's unconventional planting, made conventional through the simple act of
naming, now had street cred.

The edible landscaping movement provides a similar lesson.
Confer an interesting-sounding label—"edible landscaping" rather
than, say, "veggies in the yard"—and you have a better chance of
capturing converts. Even more successful is an exotic-sounding
label—potager, for example, a label that garden history provides

for ornamental vegetable plantings. With that, the status seekers of the gardening world may even climb on board.

The chances of aesthetic acceptance are greatly improved when public landscapes lead the way, giving us a taste of redefined convention that we could emulate in our own private yards. The city of Chicago has always been a leader in this regard—planting naturalized prairie areas in public parks, for example, and native flowers along streetscapes—and the city has likewise been forward-looking in the ornamental use of food plants. In a partnership with Moore Landscapes Inc. and the nonprofit organization Growing Power, the Chicago Park District has turned an area of Grant Park (which could be considered Chicago's front yard) into an ornamental vegetable garden. With more than 150 varieties of heirloom vegetables, herbs, and edible flowers, this 20,000-square-foot planting produces thousands of pounds of food, which is donated to local food pantries and soup kitchens and sold at farmers' markets. (Between 3,000 and 4,000 pounds of produce is harvested per year, at a market value of roughly $5 per pound.) When I speak with Growing Power's Erika Allen, she is quick to tweak my terminology: "It's not an ornamental vegetable garden," she corrects me. "It's an urban farm in the potager style, designed to be productive *and* aesthetically pleasing." The aesthetic value can't be quantified, but I wonder how many people have strolled through the park and seen Brussels sprouts in a new way—or, indeed, seen the weird spires of this vegetable's unusual growth habit (think tight little green bundles alternating up the sides of a thick stalk) for the first time. That the city has deemed them worthy of decorative use in a high-profile, popular park does more than change the view—it has the potential to change points of view.

Of course, not everyone is up to the challenges that early adopters face. Not everyone wants to be the first on their block with a

> Edible Flowers

ALTHOUGH THE following flowers are often treated simply as ornamental additions to the garden, they can also be eaten. Add them to salads for a decorative look and tasty flavor. Some flowers, including hyssop, lemon verbena, and violets, can also be added to desserts such as ice cream.

- > marigolds
- > nasturtiums
- > borage
- > bachelor's buttons

- > daylilies
- > hyssop
- > lemon verbena
- > violets

planting that defies convention. Dealing with the sometimes negative judgements that accompany new aesthetic expressions takes guts and a strong streak of self-confidence. It's easier to fit in than to stand out. But with each additional front-yard vegetable planting—whether interspersed with more familiar ornamental flowers or declaratively different with veggies alone—the standard against which fitting in is measured gets changed, bit by bit. And sometimes in a surprisingly speedy way, since one anomalous yard can quickly lead to a changed neighborhood aesthetic.

When I went to visit the front-yard vegetable garden of Russ Ohrt, a landscape designer in Hamilton, Ontario, I was expecting that his yard would stand out a mile away. But as I walked the blocks to his house, admiring the very tidy ornamental front gardens of his inner-city neighborhood, I started to notice something unusual. Here was a fruit-laden cherry tomato plant tucked beside an equally flower-laden peony. There was a basil plantation visually holding its own next to a hydrangea. In one front yard, a quirky sculptural installation told a funny joke: balanced precariously at the top of a stand were a teacup and saucer, ready for the delicious tea party one could have just by harvesting the mint for tea and the cucumbers for sandwiches. Perhaps renegade Russ had infected the neighborhood. Perhaps they'd all taken their cue from his planting and accepted his invitation to the front-yard food-growing party.

RETHINKING WHERE IT'S possible to grow food—from hidden and surprising places to the obvious—is just one of the perceptual, aesthetic, and practical shifts that urban agriculture encompasses. Hard on the heels of this rethinking of *where,* indeed nipping at the heels, is another, equally perceptual, aesthetic, and practical question: how can we make the urban soils in these hidden, surprising and/or obvious places productive enough for the growing of food?

There's desperate irony in the fact that cities, for the most part, treat organic material—the stuff of decomposition—as a waste problem that they can't get rid of fast enough. Hauled away from the curb, materials that could give life to urban soils are instead dumped in landfills where, compressed and compacted and lacking the oxygen that fuels the breakdown process, they accumulate in smelly, lifeless layers. Some cities, of course, have composting programs and residents are encouraged to separate out their organic materials for green-bin collection. Much better than the landfill, no doubt, but this is still the logic of *away,* an out of sight and out of mind approach that removes a precious resource from the place where it is needed most—urban soils.

Even more ironic, out of sight and out of mind likewise lead to out of pocket. We pay precious tax dollars to squander and lose this precious resource; we pay for a system that encourages us to ignore and forget that we could deal with organic materials (a lot of them anyway) ourselves, cheaply and simply, using one of the most low-tech inventions ever devised: the compost bin. And then we spend more money in annual panicky purchases of bags of manure and topsoil and fertilizer potions to feed our depleted soils.

Any talk of urban agriculture or food growing in cities leads inevitably to talk of composting, because soil enhancement is the number one rule of gardening, and composting is the number one way to achieve it.

It's quite easy to get obsessed with composting. And I admit that I've been there, done that and, frankly, never want to be in recovery from it.

People laugh when I tell them that I'm an official Master Composter. It's official because I passed the exam and got the pin that I can wear at . . . well, where? State dinners? People laugh even harder when I tell them that I co-wrote a book about composting. "Yes, and what were the other nine chapters about?" Har, har . . .

When the book was published, I composted the manuscript. This was before the days of curbside recycling pick-up so my gesture was more practical than symbolic—though I did love the idea of worms eating my words.

Those of a compost-centric bent, such as myself, can go on for hours about the metaphysics of rot. When my real estate agent asked me about my religious beliefs (we'd spent a lot of time together by that point), I shocked him into silence with what I still think is a damn fine answer: I believe in compost! He thought I was joking. But I meant it: the afterlife is indisputably decompositional (whatever else it may be as well). The here and now is also indisputably decompositional.

Everything alive eventually breaks down. Rot rules. This inevitability, sad and wonderful at the same time, is what makes growth possible. Soil would be a sterile material indeed without the

115

cycling of nutrients and organic matter that results from decomposition. How often, though, have you heard a city politician or city department talk about soil?

Even cities that have embraced composting programs as a waste diversion strategy have been slow to grasp the end product part of the equation: the enormously rich potential of compost to help heal our depleted, degraded urban soils. It's one thing to very sensibly download the responsibility for dealing with one's own food scraps to individual city residents and to provide them with the tools to make this possible, but our cities could go so much further. Consider the compost needs of community gardens, for example. On this scale, the gardeners could be begging and borrowing organic materials to feed their bins and still not be able to produce as much compost as they need. How could cities better facilitate the transfer of waste to resource? How could cities better deliver the compost produced from yard waste collection to the gardeners who need it?

A nonprofit group in Toronto, FoodCycles, has decided not to wait until better systems are in place and has taken matters into its own hands. Or rather, into its own bins. On an acre of land that the group has leased from Downsview Park—Canada's largest urban national park—they have set out to prove that a midscale composting facility can be effectively managed in an urban environment. Accomplishing an impressive amount in their first year of operation, FoodCycles enlisted a large greenhouse for intensive vermicomposting and salad greens production in the summer of 2009, and planted half an acre of vegetables in rows spreading out from the greenhouse doors. When I visited in mid-September, the field was a flurry of activity as energetic FoodCycles volunteers swiftly moved from row to row, pulling scissors from back pockets and snipping purple basil for one customer, rainbow chard for another. It doesn't get fresher or more local than this—I was just one of a dozen people who were shopping in the field, pointing to the cabbage we wanted for supper, tasting the difference between two varieties of spinach before deciding which one to buy. "Here, try the arugula," urged Rebekka Hutton, one of the FoodCycles founders, "it tastes like arugula is supposed to taste, not like the stuff that *looks* like arugula but has as little flavor as head lettuce." Puckering from the intense peppery taste, I bought a bagful.

As cars whizzed past on the busy road just 100 feet away, FoodCycles volunteer Sunny Lam explained the group's vision, his arms waving in the air, rarely at rest. (It occurred to me, as Sunny outlined their work, that "rest" wasn't part of their vocabulary—most of the volunteers have full-time jobs and this is a project of passion for them.) "It started with the soil," said Sunny, "and it led to food, but we're here for the soil, not just the food. When we take food but don't return the 'waste' to the soil, it's like stealing the blood from the land. By composting, we're returning that to the earth."

Worms do the returning work. Inside one of the greenhouses is a series of vermicompost bins and thousands of worms. Their nutrient-rich castings (the vermicompost) are harvested from the bins and mixed with coir and peat moss, which is then used as the growing medium for salad greens grown in trays on top of the worm bins.

"What people call waste is really gold in disguise," says Sunny, as he shares the group's plan for scaling up. There's the 100 tons of food waste generated every week at a market on the other side of the park. There are the local restaurants and coffee shops offering their food scraps and coffee grounds. There's the fruit juice manufacturer offering their pulped waste. "It goes into landfill and produces methane gas—twenty-five times more potent as a greenhouse gas than carbon dioxide. We could use it instead, here." But first, there's a significant hurdle for the group to overcome: in order to accept and compost waste generated off-site, they need a permit from the Ministry of the Environment, and to get the permit they need to conduct an expensive environmental assessment. Undaunted, they're working on it, and planning the details of the project's next phase: establishing midsized compost windrows for aerobic decomposition in 6-foot-high piles.

"At maximum capacity, we could create 200 tons of worm compost a year," says Sunny, "and in our windrows, about 111 tons." They plan to make it available to community gardens in the city.

It's hard to imagine a more elegant food cycle. Or convention more usefully turned upside down.

six

LESSONS OF CARE

FOOD GARDENS AS NURTURING HUBS

"IT'S A FERTILE place," says Pastor Mike Mills with a smile. He could be referring to the late-night teenage activity (of the amorous sort) in the secluded parking lot of Toronto's Advent Lutheran Church, or to the productive possibilities of the garden plots arrayed in front of us on the church grounds. The playful glint in his eyes suggests both. This is, indeed, a fertile place.

Nestled in an island of land—locally nicknamed "the peanut"—created by a split in the busy road, the grounds of Advent Lutheran Church in early spring look much like the grounds of the high-rise apartments that dominate the neighborhood. Yellow dandelion flowers poke up through the newly greening lawn; tiny blossoms on maple trees dangle from branches turning lush with leaves. But tucked within the traditional lawn landscape of this church are dozens of freshly dug garden plots. Some fan out in a circle, others line up in a row. Some are lined with wooden dividers, others have narrow paths of grass between them. In summer, all are overflowing with vegetables, herbs, fruits, and flowers.

"One day we stuck a shovel in the ground, and we never looked back," says Pastor Mills, channeling the church's speedy decision-making process into an even speedier description. "The congregation held a vote on Sunday. By Wednesday, we were mapping out plots, and by the following Sunday, we were digging." Marian Smith, coordinator of the garden, adds with a playful laugh: "We dug up the plots but we didn't start planting for ten days, so people were driving by thinking that the church was putting in a cemetery.—they thought the plots were for coffins!"

Advent Lutheran Church has deep connections with local community groups and it was through conversations with these groups and other partners that the idea of creating a food garden on the church grounds took hold in the spring of 2005. One of those groups was the Afri-Can FoodBasket, a Toronto-based cooperative food-buying club that early on in its genesis, more than a decade ago, started to help develop food gardens at various community locations. Anan Lololi, who, with his partner Tafari, cofounded the organization, speaks with enthusiasm about the church's decision to create a food garden: "They were so gung-ho. The reception we got from these folks was amazing."

"Right from the beginning, the idea was that it would be a garden for the community," explains Pastor Mills, "not just for members of the church." The church's Sunday school has a couple of the more than 100 plots, but the rest are avidly cultivated by a diverse mix of people from the surrounding neighborhood. With twenty-six different language and culture groups in the parish, immigrants and refugees from around the world make up the majority of the garden's plot holders, and the food they grow is equally diverse: Asian vegetables such as bok choy, Lebanese greens such as mulikhia, Jamaican hot peppers, and, appropriately enough, even peanuts (in tribute to the local name for this island of land in a sea of traffic).

"This area is really lacking in places to buy food," Pastor Mills points out, and the garden is an important supplement to many of the low-income gardeners' food dollars. This explains the long waiting list. Even though the number of plots has almost doubled from the original sixty in 2005, there are many more people who want space—perhaps not surprising in a community of 60,000 people that has just two local grocery stores.

"We dream of becoming a food center for the neighborhood," says Pastor Mills as he outlines his vision for an expanded program: a green roof on the building, a community kitchen, afterschool cooking classes for kids, a farmers' market... "This is a place where the community can come together, a place where people can gather."

The gathering extends beyond the garden itself. Every two weeks during the growing season, the gardeners host a potluck supper meeting at a community center. (Marian Smith notes that these dinners are like a "huge cooking competition," where everyone's culinary prowess is on display.) For the feast I visited, the shared meal was punctuated by the animation of a large group all speaking different languages. Many of the dishes—including Chinese dumplings, falafel, sticky rice, eggplant and chicken purée, spicy pickled cucumbers, and stuffed vine leaves—contained ingredients from the garden plots. Reeling from all the wonderful food, I still somehow managed to find room for the dish made from mulikhia—a spinach-like vegetable with a chewy, slightly viscid texture—which I'd never eaten before. Within seconds of hearing my delighted murmurs at the sweet and minerally taste, the gardener who had grown the mulikhia in her plot at the church offered me some of the seeds, which she'd brought from Lebanon. The whole evening was like that: discovering new flavors, sharing food, sharing seeds, sharing garden stories, urging others to try something new.

While the practical and social benefits to the local community are clear, the impact of the garden on the church has been equally strong. "There has been a real shift for the church, a change in our fundamental self-understanding—this is everyone's land, not just our own," says Pastor Mills. "This isn't a theology that's separate— this is a theology that grows out of common acts of living together."

IT'S NOT HARD to find other community hubs where the common acts of living together fit perfectly with food growing. The most obvious, perhaps, are schools. Cam Collyer, director of the Learning Grounds program of the Canadian nonprofit organization Evergreen, sees school gardens as the place where a constellation of benefits comes together to make children's educational experience—and, more broadly, children's lives—better. "From a learning perspective, school gardens are a great feature. They're rich in opportunity for kids. Kids are drawn to gardens and they discover so much about the world through that interaction."

One of the particular values of school food gardens, Collyer suggests, is that they serve an important role in the fight against the epidemic of childhood obesity: "Food gardens encourage physical activity, but it's different from push-ups or the flexed-arm hang. Gardening is an activity that can become habit-forming." Unlike most of the other physical activities promoted in gym class, gardening often becomes a lifelong activity.

"Another aspect to this is nutrition," says Collyer. "Kids who grow vegetables eat vegetables. Food gardens are an incredibly powerful educational vehicle to introduce kids to all kinds of nutritional issues. From growing, they're drawn into tasting."

They're also drawn outdoors, and for Collyer this is a crucial benefit of school gardens. "Childhood has moved indoors, and increasingly in front of electronic media. Free play out of doors is disappearing, replaced with play dates and activities almost invariably under adult supervision." School gardens, on the other hand, "nurture real opportunities for a diversity of free play to happen in kids' lives." In other words, what children get a taste of in school gardens is a bit of freedom.

Considering that kids spend roughly half of their waking hours at school, there's a lot of potential for turning school grounds into more productive learning environments. Yet according to a 2006 Evergreen report, *Growing Healthy Food on Canada's School Grounds,* fewer than 1 percent of Canada's 16,000 schools have food gardens. In contrast, 5 to 10 percent of U.K. schools and 30 percent of California's 10,000 schools have gardens where kids grow food. Celebrity chef Alice Waters, of Chez Panisse restaurant in Berkeley, California, is a high-profile champion of school food gardens, and her vision goes far beyond the planting of vegetables through her Edible Schoolyard initiative: the gardens are one piece of a larger project to embed "edible education" in the curriculum, to teach kids food literacy from field to fork.

While these didactic purposes may be attached to very specific educational goals—more exercise, better nutritional awareness, heightened understanding of food issues, for example—I suspect that the lasting value of school gardens is the stuff that can't be measured. At one of the most moving schoolyard food gardens I've ever seen, what is being cultivated is a most remarkable (and unmarkable through educational convention) lesson of *care.*

A familiar sensory overload hit me as I walked into the Catherine Ferguson Academy in Detroit, after first being buzzed in by the security guard stationed in the foyer. The enticing smells of

> Easy Edible Plants to Grow With Children

THE FOLLOWING plants are reliable performers, hardy, and relatively tough—thus, perfect for young gardeners. And, of course, they're tasty.

- > basil
- > dill
- > fennel
- > nasturtiums
- > parsley

- > Swiss chard
- > kale
- > potatoes
- > sunflowers
- > Jerusalem artichokes

- > pumpkins
- > watermelons
- > zucchinis

....

the school's lunch program filled the place and the muffled sounds of classroom activity—laughter and footfalls on hard, shiny floors—echoed through the halls. But I could also hear, in the background, an unusual sound: the sound of babies. Babies crying, babies cooing, babies babbling.

The school population of this inner-city public academy includes 300 girls, in grades 9 to 12—and 160 babies. The students are either pregnant or have recently given birth. Their babies and toddlers spend their days in the school nursery while the young women spend their days in school.

But not entirely in the classroom. They also spend their days in the barn, which the students built; in the horse field; in the chicken and rabbit coops; in the apiary; in the goat paddock; and in the vegetable garden. In other words, these girls start their mothering—their lessons in nurturing—long before their babies arrive.

"I'm attached to one of the rabbits," a student tells me as we tour the farm just outside the school door. She hopes to take "her" bunny home one day, "after my baby gets here and he's older, so I won't be so protective of him." A kitten meanders over and starts winding between our feet. "No farm is complete without a barn cat," she says, laughing, and sounding like an old rural hand.

As we pass by the chickens, she looks around, her hand resting on her belly, and says, "It's very peaceful out here." Even with the rooster? I ask. "He's quiet unless he's being messed with by a student. All the animals are peaceful, unless you do something to get them going." I had to admit, this was one of the quietest—yes, peaceful—farms I'd ever been on, and it was easy to forget that the highway was close by. Maybe it was the tractor on the school grounds that helped me to forget I was in downtown Detroit.

The school didn't set out to have a farm where a playground would normally be. "We had some vegetables growing in the garden," explains Asenath Andrews, the school principal, as she and I and the school's science teacher, Paul Weertz, have lunch at a local deli. "But then this science teacher," says Andrews, giving Weertz a ribbing, "got a couple of rabbits. And the rabbits had a horse. And the horse had a cow. And the cow had some goats. There was some serious genetic thing goin' on!"

If the farm snuck up on the school, it's clear that nobody would now want to go back. "Every time I even think of getting rid of the animals—say, having a party and eating them all," says Andrews, "I just think of this one time when I was doing a science experiment with the students." The experiment involved cracking an egg open every day to look at embryo development. One day the students got more than they bargained for—a premature but live chick, breathing but unfeathered. "We did everything possible for that chick, you wouldn't have believed it. Breathing into it through a straw. Chicken CPR. I even called in the school nurse!"

In the end, the chick died. "But the discussion those girls had, it was amazing," says Andrews. "We talked about premature babies and the lengths we go to to save them, the costs. And what

125

that means. And if there's no hope the baby will live . . . but it's *your* baby. They *felt* those issues. That's what you want in a class-room—for students to see the significance of these ideas in the real world."

Paul Weertz nods his head in agreement. As the driving force behind the school's garden, he's seen how the students are affected by caring for the plants and animals. "So many of them feel that they don't have much control—over their lives or their bodies—by the time we get to them. But when they're driving the tractor or riding the horse, they're the boss, they're in control."

The students feel a sense of empowerment and responsibility. They plan and cultivate the food crops. There's a weekly farmers' market every Thursday afternoon at the school. ("We've watched the food grow," says one student, "and now we get to buy it and eat it.") The students calculate how much money the garden yields per square foot. They extract and bottle honey, which they sell; they make cider from apples, which teaches them about added-value production. Although the school doesn't get any extra funding for the farm program, they manage to make enough from the market to hire a couple of students who need extra money for the bus fare to get to school. "Another school might have a football team," says Andrews, "but we use that discretionary money for the farm." She adds that they sometimes have a little trouble finding money for chicken feed . . .

Andrews says this without rancor or complaint, but I can't help feeling a shiver of exasperation on their behalf, that sometimes they have to scrounge a bit of money, mere chicken feed really, for their chicken feed. To shake the feeling, I focus instead on some-thing Paul Weertz has told me in his practical and visionary way. He farms a field of alfalfa—7 acres, 4 miles away, on Detroit's east side—and harvests 1,000 bales of hay for the school's animals. I imagine him riding the school tractor across town on the city's streets. "Every farm needs a tractor," he says.

Maybe every school needs one, too.

I THINK I now have at least some idea of what a stampede sounds like: it sounds like sixty grade 7 and 8 students stomping down a flight of stairs, then running along the basement concrete-block hallway of a big old school in order to get to the cafeteria. I remember what that teenage hunger felt like. What I don't remember is good, healthy, home-cooked food at the end of the hallway sprint.

These students, though—most running at full tilt, some skipping, one timing her steps to a chant of "quick, quick," said to no one in particular—are racing toward a meal that is one part lunch and one part radical (and radically simple) experiment: "We're proving that kids will eat good, healthy, nutritious, home-cooked meals full of fresh fruits and vegetables," says Debbie Field, executive director of FoodShare, the nonprofit organization behind the project in the west end of Toronto. When FoodShare, which has its offices in the school, was approached by a couple of parents to start a cafeteria for the Collège français students, the organization jumped at the chance, seeing the cafeteria as a logical progression from its work to create a community food hub. Following a focus group with the students ("the main thing for us is always community development," says Field), a diverse menu was created. Lunches may be anything from jerk chicken to couscous to hamburgers, with lots of free vegetables and fruits always included. "The kids have been asking for more zucchini," says Field with a big smile.

On the grounds of the school, FoodShare has created a food-growing garden ("right outside the door," says Field) and a midscale composting operation ("steps away from residences,

127

and we've shown you can do it without smell or rodents"), and there are plans to bring beehives onto the grounds. "The next step will be to integrate food we've grown in the garden and other local food into the cafeteria," says Field. These are all pieces of a connected vision, called Recipe for Change, which FoodShare launched in 2009. The goal is that every student in Ontario will graduate from high school with a diploma that includes food literacy. "We want to embed food in the curriculum, in all courses," explains Field, rhyming off examples of the many ways to make those curriculum links—everything from mapping global food circulation in geography class to exploring issues of hunger in civics class. "Schools are the place where we can teach the new generation about food—eating, cooking, growing food; composting; keeping bees, and more—and empower youth to take action," Field enthuses. "Every school should have a community garden, a kitchen, a composting facility....And, for some, maybe even a cow or two..."

The cow detail strikes me, at first, as highly unlikely. And then I think of those stampeding students on their way to a healthy meal, loading up their plates with cucumber and cantaloupe slices. Anything is, indeed, possible.

FOODSHARE'S RECIPE FOR change is likewise a recipe for better health—at every level, from personal to community. If fast food (high in fat, salt, and sugar) is the only food that kids are exposed to at school and that parents can afford at home, the costs are borne by the body. No surprises there. And no surprises in the results of study after study, which have shown that the more people grow their own vegetables, the more likely they are to eat vegetables. An often-cited research paper on the subject, "A Dietary Social and Economic Evaluation of the Philadelphia Urban Gardening Project" published in the *Journal of Nutrition Education and Behavior* in 1991, evaluated the eating habits of families involved with the Philadelphia Urban Gardening Project, one of the largest gardening projects in North America. What they found was that the gardeners ate significantly more vegetables—and more of the truly nutritionally packed vegetables such as broccoli, cabbage, kale, and Brussels sprouts—than the non-gardening control group.

Interestingly, the gardeners also ate fewer sweet foods and drank less pop. Sounds like a recipe for a longer life. And while it's a rare kid who thinks in these terms—*please pass the broccoli, mom, it's good for me*—it's not rare for kids who garden to actually want to eat vegetables. Harried parents fed up with dinnertime battles, take note: the best way to foster a veggie-positive attitude in children is to involve them in the growing of food—at home or at school. Add the exercise value of gardening into the equation and, as studies of gardeners have revealed, it gets even better: reduced risk of obesity, coronary heart disease, and diabetes.

These personal health benefits intersect with community health. In the Philadelphia study, for example, researchers found that more than 40 percent of the gardeners shared their bounty with community organizations and churches. In spreading their vegetable wealth around, they became, as the study authors put it, "nutrition change agents in their own right." Another way of putting it might be: they were fantastic neighbors. Vegetables were the vehicle of choice, but the neighborliness was also expressed in other significant ways. The gardeners were more likely to participate in local clean-ups and beautification projects. They were more likely to take part in neighborhood social events.

Quite simply, cultivation, as a guiding ethic, encompasses more than the garden—it often extends to the community. In major and all-encompassing ways. When urban agriculture researchers

Anne C. Bellows, Katherine Brown, and Jac Smit reviewed the literature on the practical health benefits of growing food in the city, in a paper for the Community Food Security Coalition's North American Initiative on Urban Agriculture, what they found sounds like a dream come true for anyone working to make our lives better in the urban environment: "The presence of vegetable gardens in inner-city neighborhoods is positively correlated with decreases in crime, trash dumping, juvenile delinquency, fires, violent deaths, and mental illness." About the only thing missing from this list is that gardens tend to look pretty spiffy, too. I suspect that it's also key. Cultivation grows a lot more than just food. It signals loud and clear that a place is looked after—that someone cares.

Anyone who gardens knows firsthand the galvanizing effects that digging in the dirt can have on the local neighborhood, whether the garden is at a church or a school or a home. Stand in the front yard with a trowel in your hand and soon enough it's a social event. Passersby stop to talk. People you haven't seen in months appear out of the woodwork. Neighbors you've never met take the opportunity to introduce themselves and tell you their names—or their favorite method of slug murder. There's something about gardening, and the multiple necessities of caring that a garden entails, that turns private effort into a community act. And everyone benefits.

130

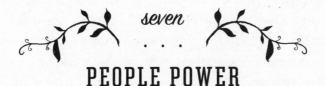

seven

. . .

PEOPLE POWER

GROWING TOGETHER IN COMMUNITY GARDENS

MAYBE WE WERE just unusually lucky, but the community garden where I have a plot chugged along relatively problem- and argument-free for about seven years before we had a situation that severely strained us all. Sure, there were minor setbacks before that, but they were of an easily manageable scale. We'd had (and continue to have in this, our second decade) the problem of pilfering. Most plot-holders have a story of arriving at the garden, ready to finally harvest that ripe tomato, only to find that someone else—surely not a fellow gardener—has been eyeing it too and got there first. Since our garden is in a high-traffic area in downtown Toronto, on Richmond Street near Spadina, and is unfenced, that's to be expected. And anyway, some of the veggie stealing is so crafty, so unlikely, that it's even possible to look on these stray events with amusement rather than outrage. One summer, a thief (who must also be a gourmet chef) dug up the horseradish root that looked so weedy most people would have been unable to identify it as a desirable edible. The cunning foodie/thief, on the other hand, spotted it, correctly evaluated its harvest-readiness, dug it up, and then disguised the act by sticking the stem and leaves, now severed from the root, back in the ground, hoping no one would notice. We wondered if a local restaurant was serving a fresh horseradish—garnished roast beef special on the menu that week.

But in year seven, the summer I was in charge of coordinating the garden, an emotional whirlwind touched down in our little project. The tornado arrived in the form of someone I'll call Nell, who showed up one day in June, and for the next three months rarely left the garden. She was clearly a troubled soul. Uncommunicative to the extreme of total silence, she nevertheless exerted her powerful personality, pulling everyone into her strange orbit.

Without warning or request, she took over one of the plots—a plot that belonged to a fellow who, understandably, wasn't happy about her intrusion. I somehow managed to keep the peace by steering Nell to an empty, available space. Soon, all manner of eccentrically combined plants began to appear in her 3-foot-by-3-foot plot: bulrushes beside a small rose bush, impatiens beside a small forest of sticks . . . She spent a good part of every day sitting on the ground, murmuring to her plants, scratching at the dirt, and picking at her scalp. I watched in alarm as, week after week, her hair slowly thinned to clumpy patches as she pulled out, bit by bit, what must have been thousands of strands. Everything she did seemed to have that same compulsiveness.

For quite a while, she recoiled from any contact, but slowly she started sending tentative signals that she was ready to respond to my overtures. Handwritten notes from Nell began appearing on the shed door. Some were written on doilies, her spidery lettering curving around the lacy edges. Others were bold and blocky, penciled onto crumpled three-ring binder pages. Some of her notes were indecipherable or enigmatic. Others were full of clear but unreasonable commands: "No bicycles allowed." One was heartwrenching: "Stop the bad man. He's hurting me."

I asked her who was hurting her, unsure of what I should or could do. Was someone assaulting her as she slept at night on the pebbled path beside her plot? Not at night, she said, during the day, every day, the bad man hurt her. I'm here most days, I said, if you see him when I'm here, show me who he is. She pointed to the two older and somewhat rough-looking men who were sitting on the rocks at the far end of the garden. I'd seen them often; they were a fixture in the garden that summer, sharing smokes and bottles. And I'd often *heard* them: one of the men had Tourette's syndrome and regularly erupted into loud cursing. Is that the man? I asked Nell. Yes. Does he hurt you? Yes, he says bad things to me, make him stop saying bad things to me.

And so, in a conversation I never could have predicted, I said to the man with Tourette's syndrome that he was upsetting Nell, who stood beside me, a quiet waif shifting her weight from one army boot to the other. When he said that he couldn't stop it, couldn't control it, I said to Nell that he meant her no harm, if that was any help to her. She nodded, glancing up at him briefly, and then she returned to the circumscribed safety of the world she controlled, her own plot. I hoped it felt a little bit safer.

If community gardens are like mini-ecosystems—each person filling a niche, each person contributing something to the functioning of the whole—the ecology of our little garden was sent spinning the summer that Nell arrived. She was a daily and constant presence that many of us found difficult to absorb. Some felt threatened by the demands she made, reading the arbitrary instructions on the signs she erected throughout the garden as hostile. Others felt unsettled by the unspoken force of her dark moods, which could cast a shadow over the whole garden. Sometimes it seemed as if there just wasn't the psychic space in the garden for anyone other than this small, silent but intensely spirited young woman. A couple of gardeners retreated, finding it, understandably enough, all too much.

But slowly, as in any ecosystem, the community garden began to adapt to and accommodate the changed dynamic launched by Nell's arrival. Everyone chose their own way to cope—either talking to her or not; making small gestures in her direction or avoiding her altogether; behaving as if things had changed or behaving as if it was business as usual. And somehow, out of the messy jumble of differing emotions and differing reactions and differing strategies, the bonds that held the garden together got stronger. We were forced to look deep into what we wanted our community garden to be. Although we didn't do anything as formal as hold a special meeting to discuss what was happening, we did, in a sense, negotiate. Through the countless acts of simply continuing to garden our plots, continuing to be there as pieces of a whole, the ecology of the community garden came to be defined as much by Nell's niche as by anyone else's.

But Nell disappeared as unexpectedly as she had arrived. One day in September, she was just gone. Over the winter, the snow flattened the bulrushes in her plot. In spring, as chives and pea shoots started to green up throughout the garden, Nell's little space stayed bare. Until the day when she was back. Wearing those same sturdy black boots but with a head of hair that looked healthy and full, Nell prepared her plot for another planting.

In the years since then, I've never asked her where she was that winter, or where she spends her days now that she no longer spends them sitting by her plot. That may be a conversation for

134

the future. In the meantime, the two of us exchange hello's and how are you's on the rare occasions when we're in the garden at the same time. She always smiles that sweet and dimpled smile of hers and tells me that things are good.

COMMUNITY GARDENS MAY be centered around the activity of growing food, but many of the most powerful and lasting effects of these gardens have less to do with vegetable production and much more to do with social interaction and growth. I'm convinced that one of the reasons is that community gardens, while functioning in the public realm, are also very intimate spaces. Where else, in public, do we carve out such declaratively personal territories of individual expression and creativity? There's a kind of blurring of boundaries that can lead to all sorts of surprises and struggles and unexpected solutions. Consider, for example, the day one of the gardeners arrived at our community garden and found not one but two fellows who were, shall we say, over-refreshed from their liquid breakfast, and actually bathing in the large watering trough. (She declined the invitation to join them in their alcohol-fueled ablutions.) Rarely does public life get more intimate than this—a park with a bathtub.

135

Community gardens are, essentially, participatory landscapes, places where people shape the shared resource of public land. There's privilege and responsibility attached to this, of course, and plenty of opportunities for conflict. Whose vision wins out in battles over competing demands and priorities is a question whose answer will only ever be as good as the community process that is engaged in order to come to a resolution. And, as in most community processes, shortcuts rarely work.

I saw this firsthand in the ruckus that ensued when a Toronto group put forward a proposal for a community orchard in a midtown Toronto park. The local councillor organized a meeting to discuss the idea, having caught wind of some grumbles of opposition. As I entered the meeting, after first being frisked by a security guard, I suspected that the evening was going to be less than convivial. Indeed, I got quite steamed when the holstered guard rooted through my purse and held up my metal water bottle with suspicion. (How had I managed to make a wrong turn and end up at airport security?) The emotional temperature inside the room was even steamier.

A local group called Growing for Green had organized an initiative to plant fruit trees in Ben Nobleman Park, across from the Eglinton West subway station. (Imagine emerging from the subway after a long workday and picking a pear for the walk home...) The group had solicited many willing and enthusiastic volunteers to carry out the project, offered workshops, held a meeting to discuss their plan with locals, and enlisted the donated labor of a landscape architectural designer to draw up a professional plan. On this warm, late April evening, as cherry buds were just starting to burst into blossom all over Toronto, the Growing for Green team had gathered again to hear the community's response.

"Someone with a beautiful fantasy convinced a city councillor of this beautiful fantasy," said one resident, with anger seeping through his irony. "Our children's clothes will be stained with cherry juice," said another. "Coyotes and foxes will be drawn to the orchard and run into traffic!" "We'll have roadkill!" "Rats and mosquitoes will infest our neighborhood." "Our taxes will be hiked to pay for water to keep the fruit trees alive." "Has a cost-benefit analysis been done?"

In the face of this opposition, Growing for Green called various experts up to the front of the room to address some of the residents' concerns. A health researcher talked about the safety of eating fruit from city trees. A playground designer talked about the need for children to engage with nature wherever they live. A horticultural supervisor from Toronto's Parks, Forestry, and Recreation department talked about the maintenance work the city would do to look after the trees. A representative from Not Far From The Tree—a nonprofit group that harvests excess fruit from people's trees—talked about the dozens of volunteers willing to pick the orchard's fruit, keep the ground free of rotten plums, and distribute produce to a food bank.

Even so, by the end of the meeting, when the councillor asked if any of those opposed to the community orchard had been swayed by what they'd heard (and, in particular, by the pro-orchard team's willingness to reduce the number of fruit trees from the original forty to twenty-seven), no hands went up. "Everything has an element of controversy," mused the politician. "The question I need to answer at the end of the day is: is this in the broad community interest?"

Four days later, the councillor produced his answer. Ben Nobleman Park would get its community orchard, but not without a political sleight of hand engineered to appease: the city would plant fourteen fruit trees and nine flowering and shade trees. "You may be asking what the difference is between fruit and flowering and shade trees," the announcement read. Well, just the name apparently. In the compromise plan for the park, the pawpaw trees and serviceberries—tasty fruit trees both—were repurposed as non-food-related flowering and shade trees. The orchard would still be an orchard, but some of the fruit trees were demoted through a change in label. As the councillor's announcement put it, "They do have small fruits which usually are eaten by the birds before any human gets them." The message? Those opposed to the community orchard would have nothing to fear, because this garden project would bear fruit and grow food for the birds. In this one small battle, the fruits of victory tasted rather bitter.

What drove the community's fear and anger in response to the

137

orchard? Why did the proposal to grow food in a public park meet with such reluctance? Sitting in that high-tension meeting, I had the distinct impression that two cultures were colliding: it was as if convention was on a collision course with possibility, established ways versus something new. Convention dictates that a park playground is made up of swings and teeter-totters. Possibility suggests that kids can have just as much fun in a grove of fruit trees, finding imaginative ways to play and, yes, maybe getting cherry-stained in the process. Convention dictates that food growing is a private, not public, act, something to be tucked away in backyards. Possibility suggests that placing food production in the center of our community's public places is nourishing—for both the body and the soul.

Fortunately, in cities across North America, possibility is gaining ground.

THE FORMS THAT community gardens can take are as varied as the communities themselves. Most are centered around food production, though some projects are focused on different goals such as naturalization using native plants or habitat creation using wildlife-attracting plants. Some gardens are divided into individual plots, with each member responsible for their own area, while others are gardened collectively, with everyone looking after the whole communal space. Some grow food just for garden members; others for donation to the community. One Vancouver community garden includes both: along with members' plots there's a "public food border" that anyone in the neighborhood can harvest from.

Many gardens combine a variety of approaches. At my community garden, for example, the roughly 30-foot-by-90-foot growing area is divided into forty individual plots (yes, forty—we pack a lot in), but there are also three small areas of native plantings that are collectively maintained: prairie grasses at the south end of the garden bordering the sidewalk, meadow flowers and indigenous shrubs in a narrow strip running the length of one side of the garden, and a woodland planting of trees and groundcovers creating a shady retreat at the north end bordering a laneway. The diversity reveals just how much can be accommodated in an average-sized downtown lot.

Community gardens often take root on publicly owned land, when an individual or group approaches officials with a vision of how that land might be used to create an amenity cared for by the community. Some cities even have community garden departments, usually within the parks division, and a clearly established process for developing the gardens once a community expresses interest. Other cities take a more proactive approach, actively searching for community groups who are willing to initiate projects on land the city has deemed appropriate for gardens.

The community's involvement likewise varies. At one end of the scale are allotment gardens, where the city manages a permit system and individual gardeners apply for a plot. These are almost like backyard rentals, the only difference being that the backyard happens to be on public land. While a strong sense of community might develop around such gardens, the allotment model is very much based on a structure of landlord and tenant rather than on community "ownership" and management. As well, since allotment gardens are often sited on "excess" municipal land, which isn't necessarily in residential communities or close to municipal services such as transit, access to the gardens can be difficult for those without cars. Thus, in some locations, allotments can seem more like commuter gardens than community gardens.

The allotment movement arose in England in the 1800s, in response to the enclosure of public land and increasing migration

> Supportive Gardening

THE SPIRIT behind community gardens isn't just about growing plants together on a shared piece of land. It can also take the form of what might be called "socially supportive gardening." Meeru Dhalwala, for example, started a vegetable gardening club in Vancouver in 2009, putting the word out through an article in the *Vancouver Sun*: "I don't want to be a solitary gardener. I want to use gardening as an excuse to meet more people in my community and give and receive for free what we grow. My only problem is that I know nothing about gardening." More than 100 members signed on and Dhalwala's club, VanGrow, consisting of new gardeners, experts, and all those in between, has become a hotbed of activity: "Our group is mostly based on bartering knowledge and physical help. For example, I had a shiitake mushroom log inoculation picnic at my house for about twenty-five members of VanGrow. I went out and bought the shiitake spores, two members secured the alder logs for everyone, three members brought their drills with the right bits, another brought dessert, and I provided a vegetarian curry and rice lunch." Other activities the group is planning include local farm visits, movie screenings, and seed exchanges. Gardening is the vehicle, community the result.

of landless rural people to cities. Legislation in 1845 (the General Inclosure Act) mandated that parcels of public land be reserved for individual food-growing use within the community. With the Small Holdings and Allotments Act of 1908, it became mandatory for local authorities to provide rental allotments to the urban population. The stridently political nature of the historic allotment movement can be seen in the fact that there were even "allotment candidates" in British elections—one of whom, Halley Stewart, won in 1887.

The allotment model remains strong in Britain and, indeed, throughout Europe. The National Society of Allotment and Leisure Gardeners, for example, is the voice representing more than a third of a million allotment holders in Britain. Germany's allotment holders' association has approximately a million members organized into roughly 14,000 separate associations. To say that allotment gardening has a strong tradition and an enthusiastic following in Britain and Europe is clearly an understatement.

North America, on the other hand, has embraced a different model, one based more on community involvement and less on an allotment permit structure. In U.S. and Canadian cities, community gardens often come about as the result of a group taking the initiative to create one. The gardens thus evolve from the ground up, meeting a grassroots-expressed need. While negotiating city bureaucracy might be laborious and time consuming, it tends to ensure strong bonds of commitment within community groups and a fierce sense of ownership among gardeners, even if they don't, in fact, own the land, as is mainly the case. This fierce commitment to place can be seen over and over again in cities that have attempted to shut down established community gardens on publicly owned land, usually for the purposes of selling the land to developers.

One of the higher profile battles occurred in New York, a city with a flourishing community garden scene that dates back to the 1970s and where there are currently more than 600 community gardens. In 1998, the scene hit the headlines when then-mayor Rudolph Giuliani proposed auctioning off 114 community gardens on city-owned property in order to raise much-needed revenue. The response was instant and vocal and it reverberated throughout North America, drawing attention to the often precarious nature of community gardens' land tenure despite their clear social value. While this particular drama had a positive outcome—all 114 sites were purchased by two nonprofit groups, the New York Restoration Project and the Trust for Public Land, which now administer the gardens—many other gardens continue to exist on borrowed time. Of the roughly 600 community gardens in New York City, approximately 200 lack permanency, their continued functioning dependent on the good graces of various landowners.

Perhaps because of their insecure status—whether or not there is an outright imminent threat—community garden organizers tend to have, or acquire out of need, political savvy and resourcefulness. When, for example, in 2008 the city of Fresno attempted to evict the Hmong Community Garden from land the group had farmed for thirteen years—4 acres of public land that provides food for 300 members of the Hmong community—organizers and supporters rallied to fight the eviction and public sympathy eventually veered in their favor. In some instances, outpourings of public support for threatened community gardens are accompanied by welcome cash: in 1984, when the city of New York tried to terminate the lease of the Clinton Community Garden in the Hell's Kitchen neighborhood and sell the land, a Save the Garden committee sprang into action, selling square inches of the garden for $5 each.

Uncertain futures due to land ownership issues are not the only threats community gardens face. At the Alex Wilson Community Garden in Toronto, where I have a plot, we almost lost one of the most basic resources required to grow food: sunlight. The threat hit us by surprise. Up until the day when a developer applied to build a condominium tower across the street, to the south of the garden, at twice the height allowed by the zoning, we had thought our garden couldn't be safer. The garden is on city property and there's a conservation easement attached to the land title that ensures this little space will be a community garden in perpetuity. (The easement was a condition of the land donation to the city by two founding members of the garden.) While the ground under our feet was locked into a garden purpose, the sun over our heads wasn't.

When the city rejected the developer's application to double the building's allowed height, the developer appealed the ruling at the Ontario Municipal Board, a provincial body that has the power to override local zoning decisions. The hearing went on for weeks and was, I'm sure, one of the stranger cases the board had to consider. Indeed, it was surreal to sit in that stuffy hearing room day after day while lawyers, consultants, and expert witnesses debated the sunlight requirements of tomatoes and garlic. It was like some weird, high-stakes gardening lesson, the results of which would determine whether our vegetables struggled or flourished.

We spent our evenings poring over the developer's sun/shade graphs and countered their statistics with our own. We pointed out that there were many ways to look at the numbers: we'd only be losing a small percentage of the available sunlight reaching the garden, but the bit we were losing meant that the sun wouldn't enter the garden until much later in spring and it would leave earlier in the fall. It was unfair, we said, to minimize the effects

143

by including in the calculation all the sunlight hours the build-ing *wasn't* blocking during winter. The shadows during spring and fall were what counted. The Ontario Municipal Board adjudicator agreed. Citing our community garden as one of the factors that led him to deny the application, the adjudicator forced the developer to redesign the building to conform to the existing zoning bylaw. The board's decision cited how the building's shadows would neg-atively affect the community garden and the shared social space of the sidewalk. The right to sunlight may not be enshrined in law, but it helped win the day in this small battle.

Our garden had a civics lesson in city politics and provincial decision-making, and we were surprised to discover that tomatoes and garlic can sometimes sway both.

It's been a long time coming, but in the decades since com-munity gardens first took hold in North America in the 1970s, many cities have started to move beyond simply tolerating them to actively promoting and facilitating their development. (Amer-ican Community Gardening Association Board member Betsy Johnson estimated in 2007 that there were approximately 18,000 to 20,000 community gardens in the U.S. and Canada, a num-ber that the ACGA says has since "probably grown significantly." The National Gardening Association estimates that a million U.S. households gardened in community garden plots in 2009.) What's interesting is that communities have been taking the initiative and that cities are now playing catch-up—it's a good reminder that the long, slow, steady slog of grassroots action can, indeed, lead to change. And sometimes the less patient approach of guerrilla action does the trick.

The city of Montreal provides an instructive example of the progressive things that can happen when both tactics fortu-itously collide, and when city governments take their cue from

> Starting a Community Garden

M OST SUCCESSFUL community gardens start from the ground up, not from the top down. They grow and are sustained by the desires of a community to garden together in a communal space. While one person, or a small group of people, may take a leadership role, many hands are needed to make the project work. Here are some tips on how to get started:

> Gauge community interest: ask around, put up flyers, call a meeting, see who comes.

> Identify possible locations: anywhere from a neighborhood church or community center to a local park.

> Decide on a working model for the group and for the garden. Clarify how you want the garden and the group to work.

> Establish a clear plan of action: delegate responsibility for contacting the site owner with your vision for the space. Anticipate all the questions that might arise and prepare answers in advance.

> Find allies in your community—in the parks department, for example, or in the municipal government (your councillor, for instance), or within community organizations who may be able to help.

> Research what resources you can get for free—including soil or compost from the city, tool donations from local gardening businesses, and grants from social service organizations.

> Hold meetings. Hold more meetings. Recognize that getting a project off the ground (or, rather, into the ground) may take a lot of time and effort. Bring cookies to meetings—baked goods are motivating.

citizen action. According to the 1994 International Development Research Centre's *Cities Feeding People Report 8,* the roots of Montreal's city-supported community gardening program can be found in the guerrilla spirit of some unsanctioned, rogue gardeners: "When Italian and Portuguese immigrants initiated illegal gardening in North Montreal in the early 1970s, the city attempted to regulate and organize community gardening." Rather than fight it, the city saw an opportunity to formalize a structure for an activity that communities were doing anyway. The result: Montreal has the largest community gardening program in Canada, with more than 6,000 plots, approximately 10,000 participants, and more than 30 acres of community gardening space throughout the city. The Department of Parks, Gardens and Green Spaces supplies the gardeners with soil, compost, manure, sand, picnic tables, hoses, water barrels—and sometimes even portable toilets. (As a community gardener whose time has often been cut short by nature's call, I'm extremely jealous.) The city likewise offers technical support to the gardeners, hiring horticultural animators to make rotating visits throughout the growing season and offer advice. (As a community gardener whose plot is losing the battle with bindweed, I'm jealous again.)

Beyond such practical efforts to aid the gardeners, Montreal has embedded support for community gardens in its policies: land designations, such as park zoning, protect the gardens from commercial speculation. Two-thirds of the city's gardens are protected in this way. If a garden without park zoning is forced to close, the city works to find a new site.

There are numerous ways that cities could move from tolerance of community gardening to active promotion and support, as Montreal has shown. And the most effective way is through policies that protect and enhance this activity. The Vancouver Park Board, for example, adopted an official community garden policy in 1996: if a neighborhood group expresses an interest in developing a garden, the park board will help them to find an appropriate site and assist with start-up. The policy has been effective in increasing the number of growing opportunities; in 1997, there were twenty-one community gardens in the Greater Vancouver region (plus five in development and five in the planning stages); today, there are more than fifty, and plans for even more. The city set a goal of creating 2,010 new community garden plots by the time the 2010 Olympics were launched in Vancouver, as a permanent legacy of the sporting event. Connecting garden goals with dates in the calendar could even be called a budding trend. The Calgary Food Policy Council is calling for 2,011 new gardening spaces by the year 2011 and has identified the city's indoor pedestrian skywalk system—all 16 kilometers of it—as an urban area with greenhouse potential. And in London, England, mayor Boris Johnson has launched a project for 2,012 new food gardens by 2012.

Toronto is another city that has entrenched community garden promotion in its official policies. With more than 100 existing gardens (roughly half on city lands) gardened by approximately 5,000 people, the Toronto Environment Office recently allocated $170,000 toward the installation or expansion of school food gardens and community garden projects. Interestingly, these projects are being spearheaded by two departments that aren't immediately obvious as garden champions: Toronto Community Housing and Toronto Public Health. Yet their involvement signals that the city "gets it." Community gardens are invaluable tools for enhancing the livability of neighborhoods and for improving public health. (Indeed, the head of the Toronto Food Policy Council, Wayne Roberts, has called urban agriculture "the new frontier in public health.") Hence, in 1999, city council adopted the Community

Garden Action Plan, which calls for at least one garden in every ward. Of course, the true test of the effectiveness of policy goals is on the ground: there are still nine wards in the city without community gardens or allotment plots, and seventy outstanding requests to start new gardens.

It's hard to imagine another single effort that cities could make to have such a broad and positive impact on the personal and community lives of their citizens. (A headline in the internet journal the *Tyee* referred to community gardens as "social fertilizer.") The documented benefits that community gardens have for every aspect of our individual and social spheres touch on just about every goal we could hope for: healthier people with more nutritious diets and more active lifestyles, thus taking some of the burden off the health-care system; stronger, more closely knit communities, thus mitigating the often isolating nature of urban life; empowerment of those with limited resources to meet some of their nutritional needs and to develop skills, thus reducing their dependence on social services; more people actively engaged with public places, thus enhancing community safety through more "eyes on the street"; public participation in beautifying neighborhoods, thus taking some of the financial burden off city departments; collective environmental action to preserve urban green space, thus increasing biodiversity . . . What other relatively low-cost initiative has the physical, mental, social, and environmental benefits that community gardens do?

Clearly, I'm a convert, but I wasn't convinced through studies and research and theories and speculations. I was convinced by Bosnians.

THE HIGH NOTES of a flute whistled through the air. A breeze ruffled hats and skirts, and brought some measure of relief to the crowd milling under the hot July sun. With hands connected, grandmother to grandchild, father to daughter, neighbor to friend, the group gathered in a circle, and slowly, deliberately, said together the word "peace." You could tell that they meant it.

We were gathered in a west-end Toronto park, home to the New Horizons Community Garden, on the garden's first anniversary. For a year, a group of Bosnian seniors had been growing food at this garden and sharing picnics.

If you added up the years represented by those standing in the circle, you would probably lose track somewhere around 1,000. If you added up the years of war and dislocation represented by those standing there, you would probably lose heart even faster. But the animated faces and the food weighing down the tables made all that—the traumas of war, the trials of immigration—seem very far away. We were together to party.

Like many community gardens, the Bosnian seniors' garden, New Horizons, represents the hard work of a handful, is supported by dozens, and is enjoyed by countless more. The seeds of the garden idea were planted by Miodrag Zakonovic, a seventy-year-old Bosnian agronomist who left Sarajevo for Belgrade when the war started ("with only my clothes"), then followed his son and daughter to Canada when the NATO bombing began in Belgrade: "I came here like a visitor, only six months, but I stayed." Miodrag brought his love of digging in the soil and his enviable work ethic with him, immediately volunteering for numerous food-related and gardening projects in Toronto. He joined an environmental group, helped with a composting project, and organized a small group of volunteers to work in a children's garden at a local park. ("I was training them for the future," he told me.)

During a tour of Toronto community gardens a few summers ago, Miodrag decided that he wanted to start a new community

149

garden—as he put it, "for people of my country." He approached
Julia Huterer, executive director of the Multicultural Association
of Bosnian Seniors and their Friends, and a plan was hatched: they
would create a garden for the multiethnic members of the association—immigrants from the former Yugoslavia—where the seniors
could grow food and meet socially.

The timeline between garden idea and plants in the ground
can often stretch to years, especially when a community group
envisions a garden in a public park. The layers of necessary
bureaucracy can seem overwhelming. The New Horizons garden,
however, was fortunate to have the committed energy of Zora Ignjatovic supporting the project. A Serbian immigrant who came to
Toronto more than fifteen years ago and, like Miodrag, an agronomist, Zora exudes the quiet can-do spirit of someone determined
to turn trauma to hope. Her experiences—losing her home, losing
her country—are always close to the surface.

Zora has had her hand in many of Toronto's food-related
nonprofit groups and community gardens (as Julie Huterer puts
it, "what we say about Zora: we've never seen a bigger worker in
a smaller woman"). She has worked closely with the city's parks
department and knows how to navigate bureaucracy.

Very quickly, with Zora's help, the New Horizons garden had
a home in Tom Riley Park, in the west end of the city, close to
an apartment complex where many of the Bosnian seniors live in
social housing. City staff prepared the soil, built a protective fence,
and supplied a large water tank. On June 2, 2007, the first vegetable seedlings went into the ground.

Zora wasn't at the garden for this groundbreaking event. But
she was somewhere closely connected: she was traveling through
Bosnia, visiting community gardens. I was with her on this trip.
We visited one garden after another where people who less than

a decade ago would have been facing each other with guns were now growing food and cultivating peace through the slow, necessary labor of one person and one plot at a time. Our guide for this tour, Davorin Brdanovic, who coordinates a reconciliation garden project in Bosnia, put it best: "Yes, one gardener is Muslim and one is Serbian, and they fought on different sides in the war, but when they're playing chess in the garden, what are they? They are gardeners." Then he added, with a wry grin, "The only fight is over who has the biggest carrots and tomatoes."

Zora and I visited gardens surrounded by yellow police tape that warned of land mines (people advised us—nonchalantly—to avoid walking in tall grass). We visited gardens where, close by, mass graves had recently been found. We met a young man so shattered by the war that he didn't speak for many years; he sat in a room listening to fifty different radios. But when he showed us his garden plot, he released a torrent of words. We stood at the site of a prison, where people incarcerated for murder gardened with members of the nearby community, as planes from the Sarajevo airport roared overhead. We met a Roma woman who supported her brothers and sisters with food from her community garden plot, proud that they didn't need to beg. And in the midst of it all, we sat at tables loaded with fruit and cookies, tea and cherry juice, while people told us their stories—every story beginning with the war, then slowly moving to the daily wonder of seeds, water, and soil.

A year later, at the first anniversary party for Toronto's New Horizons Community Garden, I was transported back to the community gardens of Bosnia: the same outdoor tables laden with cakes and cookies; children racing through the garden rows, preened by proud grandparents; cherry juice served in plastic cups and wafers with pink creamy mousse inside. I spoke in gestures with seniors who were shy about their English skills and listened

151

to a former policeman from Belgrade who was now holding everyone rapt with his joke-telling. The line separating here and there dissolved.

Tended by the doubly displaced—former citizens of a former country—the New Horizons Community Garden is a place where a new home is planted and an old home is never far away. Each vegetable, fruit, and flower in the carefully weeded rows bears a label with two names: *blitva* and swiss chard, *kupina* and blackberry, *neven* and calendula. Just as each gardener holds tight to a paired identity, each plant has two names. Names and introductions are almost inevitably followed by a country of origin—Serbia, Croatia, Bosnia—and sometimes a city—Sarajevo, Belgrade, Novi Sad, Split, Doboj. And then, just as inevitably, there are familial bonds that complicate clear divisions: an elderly Serbian-born father with a Bosnian-born daughter with a Canadian-born child now reaching for the balloon tethered to the top of a bean pole. The horizon isn't a straight line in this garden—it's a circle that enfolds.

WHAT I EXPERIENCED touring reconciliation gardens in the former Yugoslavia, and then again at the Bosnian seniors' garden in Toronto, is that the growing of food is one of the most powerful ways to bring people together. Cultivation creates bonds that can return us to the basics and take us beyond conflict—to the essential things that remind us of common purpose.

Time and time again in community gardens, I've witnessed a kind of casual (or, in the gardens of Yugoslavia, a hard-won) embrace of difference, a slide into comfortable ordinariness where differences of class and ethnicity and age and history and all kinds of personal circumstances seem irrelevant to the task at hand: the collective cultivation of food. When I visited an African community garden project in Toronto, it was at the invitation of a

Trinidadian; all the plants were named and described to me by a Somalian who was waiting for her Turkish volunteers to arrive.

Soil is fertile, unifying ground for communities. In the garden, we nurture. And growth takes many forms.

eight

ROGUES ON A MISSION
GUERRILLA GARDENING AND FORAGING

I FELT QUITE FLATTERED when asked to create a guerrilla garden as part of the Artists' Gardens project at Harbourfront, a
large cultural complex that hugs Toronto's waterfront. So flattered, in fact, that I decided to ignore the conceptual contradiction
at the heart of the commission. "Umm, the thing about guerrilla
gardens," I pointed out to Patrick, head of visual arts, "is that one
does them *without* permission. It's not really a guerrilla garden if
you're asked to do it." But the prospect of being paid a small fee to
garden trumped the contradiction. I jumped at the offer.

Patrick and I toured the Harbourfront grounds, scouting
for possible sites. I was immediately charmed by the potential
of a large, open grassy area, a kind of commons. Incongruously,
plunked down in the grass was a functioning pop machine,
exposed to the elements, and it seemed to me that a food garden,
perhaps with its very own ironic dispensing machine, would be
the perfect guerrilla addition to the commons. "Not possible," said
Patrick. The powers-that-be would never go for it.

With rogue garden dreams slightly chastened, we walked to a grassy knoll close to the lake. The regularly spaced trees on the gentle hill were just leafing out as I tried to regale Patrick with my garden vision: "Watermelons everywhere! Sprawling up and down the slope! Juicy globes of surprise!"

"Not possible," said Patrick. "The maintenance folks who cut the grass would never go for it." So much for subversion. This guerrilla garden was going to be circumscribed by lawn-mowing constraints, or it was not going to be at all. And so I accepted the unpromising site offered—six desolate concrete planters in front of a derelict building, blocks to the west of the other Harbourfront Artists' Gardens, an orphan, really—and compromised with a definitional trick. Mine would be a *demonstration* guerrilla garden, a planting that gestured to the guerrilla spirit while serving an educational purpose as well. I would plant the hardiest of native meadow species and the strongest of heirloom vegetables. In this bleak and inhospitable spot, my garden wouldn't be that much of a conceptual stretch after all, since guerrilla gardeners excel at transforming neglected, abandoned corners into places of growth.

There's something surprising that happens when you appear with trowel, watering can, and tomato seedlings and start digging in a public place. Especially if you're not wearing the uniform of city maintenance staff. Especially if you're perched precariously over the lake, hauling dirty water out by the bucketful for your planting. People stop by, hesitant at first, wondering why you're doing something so unlikely, possibly so insanely doomed to failure, as planting food alongside a public boulevard. "Are those really tomatoes?" is a question I was asked more than once. At least three people every day asked me "Can you *really* grow tomatoes in the city?" Another top-of-mind concern for summer strollers related to vandalism: "Aren't you worried that people will steal the food?" At this, I would point to the signs adorning the garden. All of the plants were labeled and the public was invited to harvest fruit, seeds, and ideas for their own guerrilla efforts. The weird thing is that, while the signs invited people to harvest food from the garden, nobody took anything. Although the garden was in one of the busiest pedestrian traffic areas in the city, and although rhubarb and strawberries were spilling over the planters and corn was calling out for harvest, nobody touched a thing. It seemed that if permission was granted, the harvesting of free food held no appeal.

But curiosity and comment certainly did. Perhaps it was the strange names on the labels of the heritage corn and tomatoes that caught people's attention and surprised potential vandals into good civic behavior: Banana Legs, Black Prince, Chocolate Cherry, Green Zebra, Strawberry Corn. Maybe these vegetables just sounded too odd to be edible. If people were uncertain about the unusual-sounding vegetables, they weren't hesitant about striking up conversations. It was the most social gardening experience of my life. Tourists, dog-walkers from the neighboring condos, locals out for a stroll—so many people stopped to talk with me as I weeded that I rarely finished the job. And everyone who stopped to talk had ideas: ideas about the prospects of successful harvest, ideas about the felonious food-stealing tendencies of their fellow citizens, and ideas about the need for more gardens like this. "The city should plant all streets with fruit trees," announced one man, "and everyone should share the harvest." Precisely.

Guerrilla gardeners don't wait for owners and officials to act. They take matters into their own hands. They scout the urban landscape for neglected sites and intervene without permission. Gardeners without land find land without gardeners—I'd say there's even poetry in the tautological simplicity of it. Even

157

though others might view this as an aggressive (or slightly impolite) erasure of the boundary between public and private or as a breach of the ownership rules on which our whole property system depends, guerrilla gardeners have another way of looking at it. We see guerrilla gardening as a kind of conversation—a communicative act sent out with hope for, but no assurance of, response. Passersby might not even notice that the garden *is* a garden, that it has been planted with intention. A few Jerusalem artichokes in a laneway could, after all, be the result of serendipity. But that's precisely part of the appeal for guerrilla gardeners. Gardens of uncertain lineage open up questions and considerations and speculation about how and why and what things grow where.

Guerrilla gardens encourage us to look at the city in a different way—they tweak our imaginations and help us discover opportunities. And once that creativity is unleashed, you never know what to expect. I certainly didn't expect that my demonstration guerrilla garden at Harbourfront would itself be guerrilla gardened. But I'm full of admiration for the sneaky rogues who discovered opportunity on that waterfront boulevard and guerrilla-planted garlic in amongst the tomatoes. Now *that* is an urban conversation that speaks volumes.

158

Unfortunately it was a short-lived conversation. Guerrilla gardens are by nature ephemeral efforts, and so was my garden at Harbourfront. In its third year, the garden was bulldozed to make way for a planting of three species of annuals. The building had been rented and gardening convention called for impatiens, geraniums, and begonias. I hope this doesn't sound like sour grapes or worse, arrogance, but I'm quite certain that no one walks by with questions or wonder or surprise as they did when the boulevard was planted with vegetables. Then again, maybe someone will take trowel in hand and guerrilla plant some garlic in amongst the geraniums?

AS A MOVEMENT with a name, guerrilla gardening got its start in the 1970s, when a group of New York City artists and activists turned a vacant lot at the corner of Bowery and Houston into a garden—a garden that still exists, the Liz Christy Community Garden—and generated a group that still exists, the Green Guerillas, who promote and support community gardens in New York City.

Most guerrilla efforts, though, lack such permanence. Richard Reynolds, author of *On Guerrilla Gardening: A Handbook for Gardening without Boundaries,* offers the analogy of "graffiti gardeners," which captures both the furtive nature of the activity and its fleeting quality. Like spray paint on walls, guerrilla gardens are often bold and hastily sketched, designed for immediate rather than lasting impact.

They also confound and frustrate clear categorical divisions. Reynolds's book includes a story about a graffiti artist in Leeds (not a gardener) whose "vandalism" and the authorities' response to it could well stand as the ultimate ironic inversion that's at the heart of guerrilla gardening. The graffiti artist's method involved stencils and scrubbing—the artwork was the clean and pristine pattern that emerged through the grime. Incensed, the local council ordered him to remove the graffiti—in essence, to "clean up" the cleaned-up wall he had exposed through his stenciled scrubbing.

Get a grip seems the appropriate response. Who can complain about guerrilla gardening when it's the most perfect of crimes? The offense isn't that someone cares enough to dig in and cultivate some neglected corner; the offense is the neglect in the first place. And that is what guerrilla gardening nudges us to confront—often through humor. (David Tracey, in his book *Guerrilla Gardening: A Manualfesto,* provides suggestions of what guerrilla gardeners might want to say if "caught" while vandalizing the city with nature: his list runs from "oops" to "Didn't you get the memo?")

159

Despite the militaristic banner, guerrilla gardening tends toward the merry and madcap rather than the shrill and moralistic. Even their weapons of choice—seed bombs—are liberating rather than threatening. Pack a balloon with time-release fertilizer, peat moss, and seeds, advised the Green Guerillas in a 1973 fact sheet, and toss these grenades of greening over fences. A Boston artist added a fertile conceptual twist: in 2005, she handed out seed bombs embedded with bitter melon seeds and invited people to launch them into neglected land. Participants were encouraged to write down those things that made them feel bitter—and toss them, too.

Even when not deliberately conceived of as art, it's not much of a stretch, I think, to call guerrilla gardening an artistic act—it's certainly imaginative. The city is the canvas and plants are the palette. And the act of gardening transforms the blank canvas of neglected corners into colorful, cared-for spaces; it focuses our attention on the neglect by turning it around. One of the most powerful inversions, memorializing and elegiac, as well as political, is the project by U.K. artist Paul Harfleet, who plants pansies at sites where homophobic attacks have occurred.

If guerrilla gardening reminds us that there's politics in plants and in the permitted uses of public space, it's often a message steeped in playful gestures. Whoever it was who planted the pumpkin seed in a street tree planter near my house surely had a well-tuned sense of humor—it's impossible to pass by the improbable globe that has grown there, silly and surprising at the same time, without smiling. And when guerrillas get together for group plantings, there's always lots of laughter. On my first outing with the guerrilla gardeners of the Toronto Public Space Committee, we were brought to our knees (okay, most of us were already on our knees, digging) by the fellow painting the falling-down fence behind our planting site. With speckles of paint splattered on his face, he was singing, to the tune of the Rolling Stones' "Paint It Black," "I see some hoarding and I want to paint it brown." As the thirty of us crouched in the cramped planting space, rear ends in the air, the seats of our jeans in each other's faces, one wag said to no one in particular, "Is this why it's called gorilla gardening?" When another of the guerrilla gardeners arrived by taxi, the group clapped—perhaps at the incongruity of her slightly fancy mode of transport to the dilapidated site. Victory fists were thrust in the air when cars honked in support as they passed our rag-taggle crew. A fellow in an SUV with a baby seat in the back even stopped and grinned ear to ear as he asked if we were guerrilla gardeners. He said he was on his way home to plant his backyard. He seemed itching to hop out and help.

My favorite act of guerrilla irreverence is that of a Saskatchewan group, who brought community attention to the potholes plaguing Highway 32 between Leader and Swift Current. The group produced a calendar, with images of people doing unlikely things in road craters—things like canoeing. In one of the potholes, someone planted potatoes.

ALL-OUT GUERRILLA ACTION is not for everyone, but if you're interested in taking tentative steps in that direction, there are lots of, shall we call them more polite, places to start. Places that are *almost* yours anyway. For example, the boulevard in front of your house. In most cities, they're planted with grass and maybe a tree or two. Whether the boulevard land is owned by the homeowner or the city, homeowners are responsible for maintaining the boulevards according to often vaguely defined property "standards." Why not take advantage of that vagueness? After all, who says that every boulevard must be planted with turfgrass? As long as your planting is well cared for and doesn't obstruct traffic sight lines, could there possibly be any reasonable grounds for the city or neighbors to take you to task?

Unfortunately, yes—not the reasonable grounds part, but the taking to task part. Etobicoke, Ontario, gardener Douglas Counter discovered this when city officials arrived at his wet-meadow boulevard planting ready to chop it all down due to a neighbor's complaint. While he held them off that day by asking a simple question that the officials couldn't answer—what bylaw rule did the planting break?—Counter was forced to spend years (and thousands of dollars) in a court battle to successfully defend his ditch meadow. In the end, the judge ruled that Counter had the Charter-protected right to garden the boulevard with plants other than turfgrass.

Beyond being mandated by the courts to tolerate boulevard gardens, some cities actually promote them. Vancouver, for example, has a Green Streets program and volunteers are encouraged to garden not only boulevards but also traffic circles and traffic bulges. The city provides soil for the gardens and orange safety vests for the gardeners. More than 300 public spaces are gardened by volunteers as part of the program. While the program discourages the planting of vegetables or fruit, I suspect that it's just a matter of time before tomatoes and blueberries start popping up in these city-sanctioned, volunteer-driven public gardens. Rhubarb and kale already have.

In other cities, citizens' groups rather than city officials take boulevard matters into their own hands. In Guelph, Ontario, a loose band of eco-activists, united under the banner of the Guelph Boulevard Club, is encouraging people to grow plants other than grass on these small plots of land. "It's a great way to raise awareness about all kinds of environmental issues," says

Gail McCormack, a founder of the Guelph Environment Network, which sponsors the boulevard project as part of its efforts to promote pesticide-free gardening. Since the group formed in 2001, there has been a steady increase in boulevard gardens in the city. "It used to be that you'd garden at night, in the dark, to stay under the radar," says McCormack. "But now it's not the taboo that it once was. It's slowly changing."

While McCormack is concerned about contamination issues, some Guelph vegetable gardeners have taken the boulevard plunge in residential areas, creating highly productive food gardens on the narrow strip of land between the sidewalk and the road. On one street, there's a boulevard garden that could almost pass for a farm stand; it's jam-packed with kale, zucchinis, chard, cabbages, eggplant, peas, peppers, carrots, and tomatoes propped up with cages.

The tomato cages haven't yet attracted the attention of Guelph officials, but in cities like Minneapolis, they're one of the reasons why vegetable gardens are not allowed on boulevards. Minneapolis has a long history of promoting boulevard gardening—its Blooming Boulevards program was started twenty-five years ago and just recently folded due to a lack of funding—but the city ordinance that allows for the planting of flowers specifically prohibits vegetables and fruits without a permit. According to Scott Graykowski of the city's public works department, "our office has never granted a permit for the creation of a vegetable garden" on a boulevard. "The reason for this is that these types of activities tend to get out of hand; residents ramp up activities by placing a plethora of garden features (such as fencing, water hoses, rocks, benches, bird baths, electrical conduit, and irrigation conduit) in the right of way. Further exacerbating the problem, plantings tend to overtake the sidewalk creating a pedestrian hazard in regards to slipping/falling. Also, plantings get in the way of opening car doors."

163

Boulevard Planting Tips

IN SOME cities, a permit is required for boulevard planting. As well, your city may have specific guidelines for boulevard gardens. Phone your councillor or your city's public works or planning department to find out if there are any local rules that relate to your plans. City officials will also be able to direct you to the appropriate authorities, so you can determine whether or not your planting will interfere with underground utilities. Other things to keep in mind include the following:

> Consider having a soil test done to determine whether or not the soil is contaminated, especially before planting food crops close to the road.

> Prepare the boulevard in the fall for a spring planting by mowing the grass very short, sprinkling compost, then adding a thick layer (ten sheets or so) of wet newspapers over the whole area. Cover the newspapers with dead leaves and compost, and water thoroughly. The materials will break down over the winter, and the beds will be ready to plant in the spring.

> Position stepping stones among your plants to prevent trampling from foot traffic, especially if the boulevard is used as a walkway or shortcut pathway from the street to the sidewalk.

> Add lots of compost, especially if the soil is compacted, which is highly likely.

> Ensure that your boulevard garden bed is level with the sidewalk and curb in order to avoid soil run-off.

> Take care not to cultivate your garden too close to the roots of any boulevard trees.

> Choose low-growing vegetables and fruits so that your plants don't obstruct traffic sight lines. Some plants to consider include: strawberries, lowbush blueberries, Swiss chard, thyme, chives, parsley, kale, cabbages, spinach, and lettuce.

> Place a 2-inch layer of mulch (straw, compost, or shredded leaves) around your vegetable planting to conserve moisture and suppress weeds.

> In the winter, apply sand instead of salt to snow on the sidewalk. Road salt can accumulate in the soil and can cause damage to plants. If you live on a busy street where city snowplows regularly dump loads of salt-laden snow onto the boulevard, it may be impossible for you to grow vegetables.

> Avoid planting perennial vegetables or fruiting shrubs, since these could be damaged during snowplowing.

> Wash all food grown on the boulevard prior to eating.

Ah yes, the car. Even in cities such as Minneapolis, which have done so much to encourage civic beautification through publicly visible gardens in front yards and on boulevards, the car trumps all. "I have seen boulevard gardens with corn stalks, sunflowers, tomatoes, pumpkins, and bean poles," says Graykowski, "and as much as I empathize with the spirit and intent, we have to ask that these plants be removed. They are not conducive to a safe and functional public sidewalk/street, especially at intersections."

I wonder if these safety concerns aren't masking other fears about challenges to convention. If rocks and hoses and benches and bird baths are indeed a problem in boulevards, why not just ban these hardscaping features rather than vegetable plants? And how exactly do vegetables on boulevards create more of a slipping/falling hazard to pedestrians than vegetables in front yards? Both areas abut the sidewalk. And if vegetable plants render the opening of car doors a problem, how have drivers long managed to cope with boulevard trees?

Such contradictions are enough to turn otherwise law-abiding people into guerrilla gardeners intent on a "plant first, deal with the authorities later, if necessary" approach.

166

Vivian Reiss, for example, has for years planted the 40-foot-by-9-foot boulevard in front of her house in the Annex neighborhood of Toronto. A painter and gallery owner, Reiss has transformed her boulevard into a colorful palette full of edible surprises. Indeed, some of her plants are so unusual, and the overall effect so ornamental, that passersby might not even be aware that the boulevard is full of food. Reiss has planted three different varieties of sorghum (also known as northern sugar cane) and broomcorn, a type of millet. She uses a pasta maker to squeeze the sugar out of the sorghum. "It's not as if I need to supply my house with sugar for the winter or anything, but I like to experiment," Reiss explains about this offbeat plant choice.

Beside the sorghum are three different amaranths, bending from the weight of seed heads laden with bright red, yellow, and white seeds. Reiss collects the small seeds—"this is really micro-milling to say the least"—and heats them up until they pop into a delicious popcorn-like snack. The tall corn plants, including a black variety with purple-streaked leaves, are more recognizably edible, to people strolling down the street—and, unfortunately, also to the raccoons. Reiss harvests the cobs early to outfox the creatures, and sometimes pulverizes the kernels into porridge. Smaller plants tucked between the rows include flax—which I at first assume is strictly ornamental, until Reiss hands me some of the seeds to eat, and I make the connection to the flax I buy from the health food store—and cotton, another of Reiss's quirky experiments.

But the biggest impact, both ornamentally and edibly, is the mini-forest of rainbow chard on the boulevard. With its thick stalks of glowing yellow, orange, and red, and its enormous green leaves, chard makes a perfect boulevard planting—it is low, glossy, and colorful, easy to grow, and each of Reiss's leaves is so large that it could probably feed a family of four.

"I do eat from this boulevard garden," says Reiss, "but I haven't planted these plants solely because they're edible. It's also because they're beautiful and educational." She delights in the kids who walk by in spring and measure the radishes daily to keep track of their progression into food.

"I'm of the 'more is more' school of thought," says Reiss, as she hands me a nasturtium flower to eat and points out that the bottom of the lower stalk contains the super-sweet nectary, while the petals are sharply peppery. "If you can walk through a garden and taste things, it just adds so much to the sensual appeal. It adds a whole other dimension." The nasturtium nectary explodes in my mouth as I nod my head in agreement. Hers is a boulevard of plenty—more is more—that looks *and* tastes very delicious indeed.

167

THE INTENTIONAL IF slightly subversive planting of public spaces with food is a useful reminder that edible plants are, indeed, all around us. We just need to look with eyes trained to edible opportunity. We just need to think like a forager.

Long associated with the back-to-the-land ethic of the 1960s and '70s, foraging is making a comeback—though in a hybrid form, an interesting mix of foodie-ism and environmentalism spiced with a touch of survivalism. Armed with out-of-print books (many of which have covers graced with a bearded, moustachioed guy—a guy who always reminds me of the dated drawings in the original *Joy of Sex*), newly hip-to-the-trend foragers are fanning out in corners of the city and finding edible plants. Ripe pickings of choice can be found anywhere anything grows—in vacant lots, along fences, on boulevards, in parks.

I suspect that the visceral appeal of foraging has its roots in our genes—an atavistic need to scavenge that in prehistory would have meant the difference between dinner and death. But there's something more, too. In a city especially, successfully hunting for food is like a combination of discovering a secret, learning a new language, and joining an explorers' club—all contained in a simple sighting of an edible green growing in pavement. The forager looks at the city through a different lens, as a place of free food with few strings attached. It helps if you have the squirrel gene.

My own squirrel-like forays into foraged urban food have yielded some unusual finds. For months I'd been eyeing a hawthorn tree that shades a sidewalk in downtown Toronto. I first noticed the tree by its stench (in flower, some varieties of hawthorns stink to high heaven). Passing under the tree one day in early summer, I wondered where the body was buried—it smelled that bad. I also wondered why many gardening books don't mention this odiferous feature. But stink aside, hawthorns earn their

> Tapping Trees

MY CHILDHOOD associations with sugaring off in the spring are all about deep-woods shacks, open fires, steaming cauldrons, and maple taffy hardened in snow. The one cup of maple syrup made by my friend Shannon from 12 liters of sap seemed very far removed from that rural tradition. City maple trees were her sap source, children from the art camp where she works were her accomplices, and four hours with a hot plate was her investment of time. A condensed cup of amber sweetness was her prize.

Municipal foresters bristle at the thought of unregulated hordes treating city-owned and city-managed trees as free-to-all for maple-syrup-making experiments. In 2009, when two Halifax residents tapped eight trees in the city's west end, the municipality's urban forester was quick to point out to CBC News that the harvesters were breaking the law and could possibly damage the trees.

Tapping trees on your own property is certainly less dicey in terms of permission, but no less dicey in terms of tree health. Before going anywhere near a maple tree with a drill bit, it is imperative to first get sound advice from a local expert. Someone at your local farmers' market should be able to connect you with a knowledgeable tapper.

169

keep as useful trees. They're very hardy in urban situations; birds love them; their flowers are pretty, white and prolific, and they produce edible fruit by the bucketful.

So, one autumn, I took a bucket down to the boulevard tree and stood on tiptoe to collect as many of the small red "haw berries" as I could reach. It didn't take long to fill my container with enough fruit to make a batch of jelly. (The fruit isn't for eating raw; it's too hard and, uncooked, doesn't have much flavor, but it is packed with vitamin C.)

Following a simple recipe I found online, I boiled the fruit with a bit of water, mashed and strained the resulting mush until it ran clear through a jelly bag, added sugar and lemon to the juice, boiled it again until the liquid thickened, then jarred it all up. The jelly jars looked like gems, the most ethereal rose color you could imagine. In truth, the jelly had more visual appeal than flavor (I found it rather bland), but on toast with peanut butter it added a sweet, pleasant kick. I labeled the jars "Richmond Street Jelly."

Other city harvesting experiments have been less success-ful. Friends still screw up their faces when I remind them of the highbush cranberry jelly I made one year and unwittingly distrib-uted far and wide before I'd tasted the stuff. It was a disaster. The smell in the kitchen (no, the whole house) produced by brewing up the berries should have been a clue. Yet another deficiency in the reference books: why don't they warn you that highbush cranber-ries release the most pungent odor of old gym socks when they're being cooked up for jelly? It took just minutes for the smell to per-meate the house and days for it to dissipate.

Once you've smelled it, there's no hope of eating the jelly without an involuntary gag—not that the flavor is as strongly eau-de-laundry-bag as the smell, but there's enough of a hint that it sends your taste buds back to the locker room. I won't be foraging for highbush cranberries again anytime soon.

But I did make dandelion wine last spring. My book-club friend Ken had been reading a weed guide and had come across a recipe for dandelion wine he wanted to try. I was game. We viewed our dandelion-collection excursion as a public service. It took us under an hour to rid an entire lawn in front of Trinity College at the University of Toronto of its weedy flowers. We steeped them in boiling water, strained the liquid through muslin, and took tentative sips. It tasted like liquid spring—like the green of asparagus mixed with something grassy. Into an antique crock it went, with oranges, lemons, raisins, yeast, and sugar. A tea towel on top and I sat back in anticipation of alchemy.

After about a day, the air in the house was thick with yeasty, fruity activity, and you could actually hear the bubbling cauldron from another room. I fretted about potential explosions, having heard too many stories of Appalachian stills, I guess. "You're making prison hooch," exclaimed my friend Brenda, explaining that Ken and I had unknowingly followed convict protocol: find any food scraps you can, add yeast and sugar, and before you know it, contraband alcohol!

When, a week later, the bubbling stopped, we bottled our vintage—Trinity College Hooch. Sadly, there was to be no refined tasting of our treasures. One by one, the bottles popped their corks. Apparently, we'd made dandelion champagne, and our vintage slowly soaked into the concrete floor of the basement.

Though my jellies and wine have been, um, interesting, I've had much better luck finding other sorts of edibles in the city. My foraging philosophy is quite simple: eat your weeds. While other gardeners are lamenting a lambsquarters takeover of their plots, I'm itching to harvest a lambsquarters bumper crop. Indeed, there's never enough of it, so I head to the parks with garden scissors and gloves. As long as I'm sticking to the weeds, I figure that the parks maintenance folks won't object.

> Edible Urban Weeds

THERE'S SOMETHING deeply satisfying about transforming weedy, reject species into feasts—the ultimate "if you've got lemons, make lemonade." Lambsquarters, for example, makes an excellent spanako-pita. I harvest as much lambsquarters as I can find and mix it up into a spanakopita filling (replacing the spinach in the recipe with the weed) that I keep in the freezer.

Garlic mustard is another tasty, foragable weed. An invasive species that messes up the ecology of natural areas—outcompeting the native flora and turning once-diverse woodlands into mustard monocultures—I'd say it's practically our *duty* to eat this bully. So every spring, I head to a local park and go on a harvesting mission, cutting off young garlic mustard leaves. I don't pull it up by the roots because that disturbs the soil and gives a boost to the thousands of mustard seeds lurking there. But cutting the plant down to the ground prevents this biennial from flowering and thus producing thousands more seeds. Fortuitously for weed eaters, repeated cutting is one of the best ways to control this invasive species.

The tender leaves of garlic mustard make a wonderful pesto, more garlicky than the basil version of the sauce and a perfect accompaniment for pasta. I make loads and freeze it for the winter when weeds, and indeed anything green, seem very far away.

Other edible urban weeds include plantain, burdock, chicory, dandelion, mallow, amaranth, and purslane.

Feasting on weeds not only offers a tasty scheme for bully reduction, it also provides educational opportunities to spread a valuable ecological message about invasive species and their effect on natural areas. Collingwood Neighbourhood House in Vancouver, for example, holds an annual Himalayan Blackberry Festival in August which both celebrates the flavor of this highly invasive scourge of natural areas and raises awareness about its environmental effects. Blackberry jam making workshops at the event spread the message.

While foraging for weeds feels to me like a virtuous activity, harvesting native plants from natural areas—urban or rural—is an ethical minefield. It's one thing to dig up ecologically disruptive species and eat them, turning a problem to culinary advantage, but it's quite another thing altogether to disrupt the ecology of natural areas by harvesting from healthily functioning plant populations. For one thing, they won't remain healthy populations for very long if everyone is doing it. There's more than a whiff of elitism to any justification that depends on the idea of, well, it's just me, it won't hurt. In case this sounds self-righteously smug, I should confess that I've taken this attitude myself on a number of occasions. There's a glorious redbud tree in a park near my house, and for many spring dinner parties one of my last-minute preparations involves hopping on my bike and heading to the redbud to harvest the prolific pink blossoms for a salad of mixed baby greens. Guests are always impressed by the colorful decoration and enjoy these little nuggets of nectar (hidden honey is released with each bite). I always try to harvest the blossoms when no one is looking, not because I fear arrest but because I don't want anyone else to copy the activity. Guilty as charged—I can do it but others shouldn't is pretty much the textbook definition of elitist posturing.

I figure that a few flowers hardly make a difference (and, in my defense, I should add that the redbud I planted in my backyard is

173

getting close to supplying me with enough flowers for spring salads), but it's another story for many of the native plants that adorn woodlands in particular. Consider how few intact forests still exist in urban areas throughout North America. Then consider the impact that even a few foragers can have on the native plants that have somehow managed to survive in cities. Fiddlehead ferns—those tasty harbingers of spring—won't last long if their young, curled-up fronds are overharvested year after year.

Fruit, on the other hand, can be a guilt-free pleasure—a renewable resource produced year after year by trees, shrubs, and vines. And our cities are laden with it, if you know where and when to look. There are foraging opportunities in parks and natural areas, of course, though in many places it's technically illegal to pick anything from public land. But if the sight of all that ripe, unused bounty nudges you into felonious behavior, fruit plucking probably won't get you arrested, particularly if you're discreet.

In some North American cities, groups of volunteers have banded together for more organized fruit-harvesting efforts. Most are polite, permission-based projects, in which trees on private property are offered for harvest by homeowners who are happy to see the fruit not go to waste. A few projects make a more political point in what might be called the underground fruit economy. A group of artists in Los Angeles, for example, posts maps on the internet of accessible fruit growing in Los Angeles, including trees that overhang sidewalks, and encourages everyone to harvest, plant, and sample public fruit. "Our project, Fallen Fruit, instigates a conversation about what's public, what's private, and what public space means," says David Burns, one of the trio of artists behind the project. Less overtly activist is the tactic of a fruit tree project in Kitchener, Ontario, organized by Karin Kliewer and Greg Roberts, who run an eco bed-and-breakfast called Little City Farm.

> Edible Native Plants to Grow in Gardens

THERE ARE many compelling environmental reasons to grow native plants (wildlife attraction, for example), and some native plants have the added benefit of being edible. Not only that, but *delicious* and edible. These are some of the edible native plants readily available from nurseries:

- hog peanut
- wild ginger
- hyssop
- wild leek
- nodding wild onion

- pawpaw
- serviceberry
- persimmon
- black walnut
- prickly pear cactus

- ostrich fern
- elderberry
- huckleberry
- sarsaparilla
- wild strawberry

A couple of years ago, they posted an advertisement in the local paper saying that they'd be willing to harvest fruit from households that had extra or were unable to harvest it themselves. "We were flooded with emails and phone calls from a wide range of people," says Karin. The list included "seniors who couldn't climb a ladder; a man who was just overwhelmed with his apple and pear trees and didn't want to harvest any more (but didn't want to see them go to waste); people who were going to be on holiday when their fruit was ripe; a pregnant mom who loved to get some fruit in exchange for us doing the picking; and even a 100-acre orchard outside the city that was going to be bulldozed in the fall, to make room for a subdivision development."

The majority of fruit-gleaning projects are, like Little City Farm's, freely exchanged, give-and-take agreements between

175

those with trees and those willing to donate labor for a productive purpose. "We'll pick anything from anyone, anywhere," says Erin Kastner, coordinator for the Vancouver Fruit Tree Project. Started in 1999, the group went dormant in 2007 but bounced back in 2008 with thirty picks by approximately forty dedicated volunteers. "We harvested almost 4,000 pounds of apples, pears, grapes, plums, and even some figs. We could have easily tripled that if we'd had more vehicles," Kastner says. As in many projects, the harvest is divided between the volunteers, homeowners, and members of the community such as neighborhood centers, day cares, and seniors' residents. "The only problems are logistical—homeowners calling us to say that the fruit is ready when it's not, or it has already fallen off the tree; or the challenge of finding coordinators for different areas every year. But we have some real champions—people are very committed to this."

Indeed, gleaners across North America are a committed bunch, devoted to using fresh and free urban resources. (Neighborhoodfruit.com lists 10,000 public and backyard fruit tree locations in the U.S.) Village Harvest, a San Francisco Bay Area project, had roughly 900 volunteers who harvested more than 173,000 pounds of fruit from 500 homes and orchards in 2009. The produce was distributed to approximately fifteen food agencies and food banks. When Asiya Wadud recently started the group Forage Oakland, in the city of Oakland, more than 200 people signed up. The B.C.-based Richmond Fruit Tree Sharing Project, which began in 2001, has harvested more than 130,000 pounds of food over the years, and, in 2008, branched out from gleaning to producing, by planting a 1-acre apple orchard. It's a logical progression; many groups begin with picking and expand into related efforts. The Vancouver Fruit Tree Project, for example, has done canning workshops in partnership with community kitchens, helping people who are overwhelmed with produce to preserve the bounty.

I suspect that a big part of the appeal of all this fruit-focused activity, along with the satisfaction that comes from foraging free treasures that would otherwise go to waste, is that it's fundamentally social and neighborly. Quite simply, it's based on sharing—sharing food, sharing effort. Picking becomes a party, the city an orchard. One person's liability—a tree dropping fruit—becomes an asset for someone else. Intergenerational bonds get forged—younger folks do the climbing, older folks get part of the reward.

"I started to see my neighborhood and my neighbors in a different way," says Laura Reinsborough who, in 2008, founded Not Far From The Tree, a fruit-scavenging collective in Toronto. "I didn't realize how many fruit trees there were in the city, but once I spotted one, I started seeing them all over!"

Reinsborough calls this putting on her "fruit goggles," and says that she now sees her neighborhood in a different way. Her group harvested more than 8,000 pounds of serviceberries, apricots, plums, and other fruit from Toronto trees in 2009, a number that surprised her: "I mean, this was not a concerted agricultural venture. This was just some homeowners saying 'oops, I've got some fruit trees I don't have any use for.' It just shows you the potential of urban agriculture." Reinsborough's eyes light up to accompany her smile—she's got her goggles trained on the 1.5 million pounds of fruit growing on Toronto's trees: "It's a very, very, very rough estimate, but just think . . ."

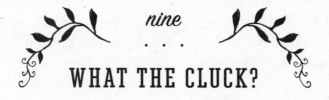

WHAT THE CLUCK?

BACKYARD CHICKENS

I MADE TWO LIFE-CHANGING decisions last winter. I decided to end my relationship with my partner of almost three decades, and I decided to raise chickens. I'm not sure which came first, the chicken decision or the relationship decision. I certainly didn't connect them at the time, though others did. My brother's reaction to my twin announcements, after the surprise had settled and there was the tiniest crack of an opening for something other than grim revelation: "What's this? Ditch the boyfriend and get birds?"

I guess I figured that if there was going to be pain, let there be poultry, too. I dove into both.

Grief quickly gives way to slapstick when you've got backyard chickens. These ridiculously endearing creatures are so game for whatever's on offer—the word inquisitive was invented for poultry, I'm convinced—that you can't help but join in with their spirit of comic adventure. Over the months of getting to know one another and growing into our respective lives in unfamiliar territory (me, newly uncoupled; them, newly cooped up in downtown Toronto), we looked after each other, these three gals and I. We didn't exactly learn to spread our wings and fly, but we did manage to jump over some barriers that at first seemed insurmountable. We clucked up a storm during those early months—mine full of emotional thunderclouds, theirs full of gawky quests. We spent our days digging deep. Thing is, I was digging for emotional clarity. They were digging for grubs.

A chicken's day and a relationship-griever's day are remarkably similar. Wake up confused and foggy at an early hour. Wander around your roomy but enclosed coop, waiting for the world to wake up and offer distractions. Peck at your food. Scratch at the ground to make sure it's still solid. Vocalize increasingly loud *bwaawks* until someone hears your call and offers what you need— company, soothing murmurs, sustenance, an open door to the world outside your head. Scoot free from the coop, without a plan or destination, and forage. Follow your friends somewhat frantically. Bob your head and cluck to yourself. Feel overwhelming gratitude for anyone who pays attention to you. Have moments of extreme withdrawal. Fear surprises, shudder at sudden loud noises, and scatter. Dig a crater in the dirt and flap as you settle in. Revel in the sun on your back. Realize you're hungry and peck at your food again, spilling more than you eat. Retire at dusk, and stay awake for hours, crouched on your roost.

Maybe I was taking this poultry-identification thing too far, viewing my life as some kind of chicken chick-flick? It was hard not to, though, when most conversations with friends and family followed a similar pattern: taking a barometric reading of my emotional state, then a segue signaling the end of wallowing—"And how are the girls?!"

The "girls" are Hermione, Nog, and Roo, each one a highly excitable creature full of personality. Hermione, an Araucana who lays blue eggs, carries herself with a most un-chickenlike haughty elegance that she manages to maintain even when doing something completely ungraceful. Such as the time she got her head stuck in a small gap in the plastic fence. I feared for her wings as I pulled her out, worried even more that her neck couldn't take the tug and I'd be left holding a lifeless sack of feathers. Or worse, that her ending would be that clichéd trope—a chicken with its head cut off. Phew, she came free, ruffled her shiny dark feathers (streaked in black and brown and rich gold), and sauntered to her food dish with a composed "that was on purpose" glance my way.

Nog is the smallest of the crew—a burnt auburn Babcock—but what she lacks in size she makes up for in eagerness. "I'm here, I'm here," she calls out incessantly. It actually sounds like a bit of a wail to me, but others have commented on its soothing nature. If my little clutch has a pecking order (I find it hard to tell), Nog is at the top. She's the first one to leave the coop when I open the door, the first one to return when I come by with treats throughout the day, the first one to lay a brown egg every morning. The others don't exactly look up to her (I suspect that respectful deference is not one of the items in a chicken's behavioral catalog), but they do follow her and seem to appreciate her leadership qualities, such as they are.

Roo, a Buff Orpington and the biggest of the bunch, earns her sandy ginger coloring by being the schoolyard troublemaker (much like the ginger cats of my acquaintance). She was the first one to discover that the 2-foot-high fence I'd installed to separate the girls from the rest of my garden was actually quite breachable. She didn't exactly sail over it but she did get enough of a running start that some flustered parody of flight was possible. Plan B, installing a 3-foot-high fence, was somewhat more of a challenge for the troublemaking Ginge-a-Roo. The first time she flew the coop she was so alarmed by her freedom that her worried clucks reached me on the third floor. When I lifted up the bottom of the plastic fencing a couple of inches, she flattened herself under, then puffed herself up on the other side, preparing for more troublemaking in the safety of her home range.

In truth, though, I'm the troublemaker in this backyard experiment in urban chicken-keeping. My city has a prohibition against harboring certain animals, whether as pets, for food, or for fun. Chickens seem to be on the list, though it's hard to decipher. "Ant-eaters, kangaroos, lemurs, mongooses and elephants" are clear enough, but for birds, figuring out whether chickens fall under the prohibited category of "Anseriformes, Galliformes and Struthioni-formes" is a research project requiring a good field guide. I didn't need to check, though. I knew before I brought the girls home that they weren't allowed. But in the same way that I was ignoring the Municipal Code, Chapter 349-18 (A) (registering your cat), I was ignoring what Article II had to say about Galliformes. If caught, I would plead Latin illiteracy—*Struthioni-what?*

Hiding three chickens in a downtown backyard the size of a municipal swimming pool is actually quite easy, though. I decided not to tell the neighbors in advance, thus defying every piece of chicken-keeping advice I'd read. Notification might have sounded like a request for permission and what if they refused it? I was game for defiance of the authorities but not for outright hostility to the neighbors. Besides, I'd had enough tut-tutting from the few friends I'd told of my plan in advance, so I had a good idea of what the neighbors' reactions might be. Many people I knew seemed to have some once-removed chicken-keeping experience in their distant past, and they clucked disapproval.

"Oh, you won't believe the smell!" they warned. When I pressed for details, it turned out that the odoriferous hens belonged to an eighty-five-year-old grandmother whose coop management consisted of a once-a-year cleaning whether the henhouse needed it or not. "Oh, the noise—they make quite a racket!" Turns out the clamor was caused by a rooster, and there were no boys allowed in my club.

So I kept my hens a secret from the six people living within 15 feet of me for as long as I could. For three of those neighbors, my subterfuge lasted exactly two minutes. One minute to carry the cardboard carton from the car to the backyard. Half a minute to lift the chickens out of the box and into the coop. Half a minute of stunned silence, then three surprised hens letting the world know that they had now arrived. *Bwwaaaawk, bwwaaaawk, bwwaaaawk.* My neighbor to the south, Pete, was out in his backyard that warm spring evening with his two adult sons, Cam and Kevin. (Strangely, in the seven years I'd lived here, I had not once—*ever*—seen all three of them outside together. But, of course, on this, of all nights, a family powwow was in full swing.) As I crouched by the coop, willing the girls into silence, Cam sprang into action. "Are those chickens?!" he squawked, racing to the fence and poking his head over, a huge grin on his handsome face. "Umm, yes," I squeaked in reply. Kevin was quickly at Cam's side, the two of them now smiling in unison, delight and disbelief in equal measure. Pete, towering at 6-foot-5 and on his toes, was somewhat more circumspect. "Are you allowed to have chickens in the city?" were the first words out of his mouth. I chose to ignore the question, launching into an excited babble about what sweet, no-fuss neighbors the gals would be, peppering every sentence or two with "and there will be eggs for you, too!" This was an outright bribe. Pete looked dubious but not dismissive, and I considered that the best I could hope for, for the moment. "Let me know if they bother you in any way," I finally said. "This will only work if they don't cause you problems." Deal sealed, the three fellows retreated from the fence, Cam saying, to no one in particular and with a gentle, dreamy yearning so touching from a twenty-year-old guy, "I want chickens, too."

A lot of North American urban dwellers want chickens. No one is keeping statistics, but a revealing measure might be the popularity of the website BackyardChickens.com. The majority of North American urban dwellers are actually allowed to have chickens. Name the largest cities in the U.S. and chances are that they are hen friendly (roosters are another story, understandably). You can indulge in backyard egg production in New York City, Chicago, Los Angeles, San Francisco, Seattle, Cleveland, Miami, Atlanta, New Orleans, Minneapolis . . . the list goes on. Smaller places show their agricultural roots, too: Portland, Ann Arbor, Madison, Little Rock, Austin, Louisville, Boise, Santa Fe, Salt Lake City, and Burlington. According to Barbara Kilarski's 2003 book *Keep Chickens!*, a resident of Houston is allowed to keep seven chickens if the person is under doctor's orders for fresh chicken eggs. Even the city of Las Vegas, probably the last place that comes to mind when one thinks of urban agriculture, permits poultry.

Some of these cities are lucky enough to have supportive groups that spread the word and offer assistance, encouragement, and troubleshooting. A nonprofit organization in Portland, Oregon, called Growing Gardens conducts an annual "coop tour" event, much like a garden tour except that instead of flowers, it features feathered friends. This Tour De Coop is so popular that more than 1,000 participants visited twenty-five backyard chicken operations in the summer of 2009. The Seattle Tilth organization offers a City Chickens 101 course and a Starting With Baby Chicks course. Just Food, a New York City nonprofit organization, promotes urban poultry through its City Chicken Project. Along with publishing handbooks and coordinating a Web-based discussion group, they provide training and assistance to the roughly ten community gardens in New York City that have hens.

These groups tend to have an activist bent, not limiting their activities to education and assistance but often sliding into advocacy, especially when there's a restrictive bylaw to challenge. The Chicken Underground, a Madison, Wisconsin, group, worked to make keeping chickens legal in their city in 2004, a story cheekily told in the film *Mad City Chickens*.

Canadian cities, too, have become hotbeds of poultry promotion and activism. While a handful of smaller cities (Victoria, Brampton, Niagara Falls, Burnaby, Richmond, and Guelph, for example) allow chicken-keeping for personal use, bigger cities have been slow to jump on the bandwagon, though debates are raging. Such controversies often follow a predictable pattern, as exemplified by the issue's progress in the large east-coast city of Halifax. There, in January 2008, Louise Hanavan was ordered to get rid of her three hens (Captain Crochet, Bernadette, and Chicken). Neighbors said they were attracting rats, and the Halifax Regional Municipality took action. The ensuing outcry convinced the city to give Hanavan a one-month reprieve while the municipality invited public input. At a February community council meeting, protesters wearing T-shirts with slogans like "Urban Chickens are Cool" paraded with signs proclaiming that "Halifax Welcomes Chickens." (Hanavan took her chickens down to city hall—"the hens were good sports about it," she says.) The crowd did good-karma-inducing chicken dances, and the media had a field day. Bad puns proliferated in print: "running afoul of the law"; "it's no yolk"; "backyard chicken coops won't fly." Facebook sites popped up with petitions, the blogosphere was buzzing, and updates were Twittered. In the end, though, the order against Hanavan stood, and she moved her girls to a farm. Plans to move Captain Crochet and the gang back to

Halifax, to the Cole Harbour Heritage Farm Museum, where they would became part of an educational display on urban agriculture, didn't pan out, so Hanavan's hens stayed on the farm.

Reason rarely enters into chicken bylaw battles. A midsized Ontario city, Waterloo, is a case in point. That city's staff, with the enthusiastic support of the Waterloo Hen Association, drafted a bylaw for council's approval in 2009 allowing up to ten birds per backyard. The medical officer of health wrote a comprehensive report, concluding that "After a review of health risks, peer-reviewed literature and experiences from other health units on backyard urban chicken farming, Public Health has determined that raising chickens in urban areas contributes to enhanced urban agriculture, increased food security and greater access to local food for households who wish to engage in this activity." While acknowledging that there are risks, the Public Health department concluded that "these risks can be mitigated through sound biosecurity measures and regulatory conditions." If biosecurity is not exactly a concept one wants to consider in a backyard context, keep in mind what this scary, Ebola-ish term basically means: clean up the poo on a regular basis. But Waterloo councillors balked, rejecting the reassurances of the city's own health experts, and upheld the ban.

It seems that there's something about urban chickens that really gets politicians' goats. (Maybe they're afraid that goats will indeed by next on the urban agenda?) In the southern Ontario city of Hamilton—an industrial place that could do with a little agricultural softening of its rougher edges—the planning committee actually refused, in May 2009, to even hear a citizen delegation proposing to amend the anti-chicken bylaw, even though such committees are supposedly open to public inquiries and refusals are rare. As one councillor put it, "I'm not sure we want to go down that road, and it's not that I'm chicken, but I don't think we even want to hear a delegation about allowing chickens in the backyards of our urban area boundary." No discussion, no debate, and his motion to disallow the delegation passed unanimously.

Patricia Foreman, author of *City Chicks*, went to rather extreme lengths to try to get the city council in Lexington, Kentucky, to allow people to raise chickens. She took Attila the Hen to a council meeting, but no dice.

There have been some notable victories, however. The third largest city in Canada, Vancouver, voted unanimously in March 2009 to legalize the keeping of urban hens. Three months later, enrollment in backyard chicken workshops was booming. Can bylaw success for the Calgary Liberated Urban Chicken Klub (CLUCK) be far behind?

ALTHOUGH I PROMISED myself I'd keep mum about my chickens, not wanting to court official sanction from the authorities, it turns out that I'm terrible with secrets. The gals are companions I find impossible to keep to myself. Any excuse to spill the beans and I'm yammering away in too-much-information mode. It often takes the form of a high school sex ed class, with me in the role of nerdy, middle-aged instructor. I can't begin to count the number of people who are confused about the birds and bees when it comes to chicken reproduction. "Don't hens need a rooster to produce eggs?" is the first question almost everyone asks. (I wondered this, too, for a very long time; indeed, until about a month before I got the girls, and even afterward, I was more than a little vague on some crucial, basic biology.) When the inevitable rooster question is out in the open, that's when I go into schoolmarm mode, though I try to temper it with conspiratorial innuendo, especially if the questioner is another woman. "The gals are just like us," I

187

say, winking, "producing their eggs, ready for reproduction. No rooster nookie, no fertilized egg. So they shed them, just like us."

Biology lesson complete, the next question is usually more practical. "Are you allowed to have chickens in Toronto?" Well no, I always admit, but then I add, as if to make the whole thing less illegal, "not *yet.*" This is actually not as dissembling as it sounds. Toronto is in fact in the midst of a chicken debate, with some councillors willing to take on the battle of transforming public opinion from con to pro. It'll take a lot of work, given that most polls reveal a decidedly chicken-phobic majority. Common fears fall into predictable categories—noise, smell, avian flu, predators, rodents, animal cruelty concerns—and fuel a lot of anti-chicken outrage. Each one of these fears has room for reasoned discussion. Noise? Hens are quieter than dogs. (Roosters, it seems clear, are a noise problem and, I'd say, could and should be banned from cities in the interests of good sleep.) Smell? Not if you keep the coop clean, and it's easy enough to frame bylaws with mechanisms to deal with odor complaints. Avian flu? No less an authority than the U.S. Centers for Disease Control and Prevention has this to say: "In the United States there is no need at present to remove a flock of chickens because of concerns regarding avian influenza." When it comes to diseases, I'd put my money on a backyard-raised hen any day, compared to one raised in industrial conditions. Predators? Chances are, this is not an issue with proper coop and run protection. Rodents? Not if chicken feed is properly stored. Animal cruelty concerns? This can and should be covered under the same bylaws that protect *any* pet or wild animal from harm. And, frankly, if one is worried about animal cruelty, I'd suggest directing one's efforts to outlawing the horrific abuse of industrially raised hens.

The incensed emotion that urban chickens can arouse seems so out of proportion with the (for the most part) gentle nature of hens that it would be comical if it didn't turn people like me into outlaws. I've heard so many otherwise live-and-let-live philosophical types become rabid when the subject of urban poultry comes up. "They just don't *belong* in the city" seems to be the gist of their heated deploring. As if the rule book shouldn't be regularly renegotiated, updated, transformed, and opened up to sensible revision.

Luckily, Toronto seems willing to consider the possibility. A multi-departmental committee composed of different city departments (oh, I can just hear the "my tax dollars" complaint now—actually, I share the complaint!) is on a fact-finding mission, and all bets are that they will recommend a pilot project to test the feasibility of conducting a controlled experiment to consider the possibility of blah, blah, snore, snore . . . I mean, really, every major city in the U.S. and a bunch of smaller cities in Canada have allowed urban chickens for years, and these cities have not turned into smelly, noisy, rat-filled places. Oh wait, maybe some of them have, but you can't blame the chickens.

I'd say that chickens are, if anything, a civilizing influence. Show me a kid who goes to the backyard hen house every day to collect eggs and check in on the girls and maybe give them a lettuce treat, and I hazard you'll see a child who transfers that caring to many other spheres of his or her life. Or maybe I'm romanticizing—a dear, elderly friend, Beth, tells me of the fun she had as a child, when it was her job to collect the eggs. One of her fond memories is of getting into egg fights with friends, returning to the house all smeared and splattered with the yolks and whites of breakfast dripping down her body. Well, perhaps chickens can sometimes be civilizing as a relatively harmless aggression outlet.

I've got a modest proposal for the pilot-project-promoting politicians and bureaucrats of Toronto. Instead of spending all that money studying the issue of urban chickens and writing a report that probably won't convince anyone who is confirmed in their

189

anti-chicken beliefs to change their mind, give the money to me. I'll use it to invite everyone over for dinner, any time. Open door. Come see my girls. Sniff their coop on high alert, ready to find ripe odors, and discover instead the smell of hay. Listen with the jangliest of nerves for loud noises, and discover instead the soothing soft clucking. Hunt for vermin, and find that the chickens have eaten all the bugs. Watch for rats, and find that they've headed down the street to the much more accessible restaurant bins and garbage cans. I guarantee that anyone with chicken doubts will sit down for the communal dinner in my backyard—a dinner of oeufs mayonnaise, soufflé, quiche, and frittata followed by custard and meringue cake—and wonder what all their chicken worries were about. They'll leave the table converted, contented (egg-full bellies do that to a person), and planning their own coop. My chickens will have pulled off a civic coup.

Indeed, my girls have already pulled off a minor coup of sorts. While my neighbors to the south—Pete and his sons—were on to my backyard additions in a flash, Patrick and Shannon to the north didn't notice them at all. *For a whole month*. Finally, unable to take the suspense any longer, and worried that their lack of comment was based on severe disapproval (and perhaps even plans to phone the authorities), I approached their front door on a warm Saturday morning with one blue egg and two browns cradled in my hands. Cautiously, I asked them if they'd noticed anything new about my backyard. Nope. "I've got three chickens," I blurted, passing them the eggs. Patrick and Shannon couldn't have been more gracious. I was in a state of high anxiety, so my memory of our exchange is fuzzy, but I think Shannon may have mentioned Martha Stewart as she took the blue egg offered. Apparently Martha recommends the Araucana breed. (I feel certain Hermione would raise her beak proudly in the air at the news of being Martha-approved.)

I couldn't have hoped for a better reception. Three chickens 15 feet away for a whole month, and two of my neighbors hadn't noticed. That seems like the most convincing response to the "chickens don't belong in the city" argument I've heard yet.

That said, there are definitely precautionary measures that novice chicken keepers should take in order to keep everyone—chickens, neighbors, city officials—happy. Since I didn't take many of them myself, I feel qualified to offer advice to others. First of all, think like a chicken. Take a beady-eyed look at your yard, cunningly calculating all possible means of escape. This only applies, of course, if you're planning to allow your hens free-ranging access beyond their coop. But if you are—and in the interests of chicken amusement and occupation, I recommend that you do let them out of their confines regularly; either that, or build a very large coop, perhaps with a roof—then make sure that they *stay* in your yard.

In my case, this meant covering all small gaps in the existing wooden fence with chicken wire, an endeavor that led to many scratches, some bleeding, and much frustration with the drill. But at the end of the exercise, I felt an almost military satisfaction that I had, indeed, *secured the perimeter.* Turns out I was deluded, but that's a story for later.

Also consider the effect that the chickens—in particular, their digging, scratching, eating, and pooping—will have on your yard. On this score, I confess that I allowed poultry yearning to trump realistic appraisal in my advance planning. It didn't occur to me to wonder, until the day before I picked up the girls, just what they'd *do* to my garden. Very odd in retrospect, especially from someone whose garden is both her passion and her profession.

I'd spent years creating my backyard oasis, and it was finally looking like the lush native-plant habitat I'd hoped for. The

191

woodland section was a mass of jack-in-the-pulpits, bloodroot, ferns, Virginia bluebells, wood poppies, and wild ginger, all colorful in spring, and the meadow was up to my shoulders in summer, a riot of blooms. I imagined great chicken games of hide and seek in the foliage, and my benign imaginings allowed no hint of destruction. But there must have been some stray doubts lurking behind the rosy picture because just before D-day something compelled me to google the question "will chickens wreck my garden?" Each URL held warnings more alarming than the last: "Chickens and gardens do not mix"; "There will be nothing left where they are. No grass, no plants, no weeds, just bare dirt"; "They dig freaking craters"; and, most ominously, "The Feathered Land Shark will destroy any established flower beds." Oh dear, goodbye garden.

Just as I was weighing the lure of prospective eggs against the cost of a scorched-earth yard, a well-timed mail delivery arrived: *The City Chicken Guide: Raising Hens for Eggs in NYC,* published by the nonprofit organization Just Food. Clearly this booklet was written by some serious poultry promoters—who else could say, with a straight face, "our project has grown to include a dedicated Chicken Committee"? (Then again, poultry promoters—myself included—do tend toward earnestness. The group United Poultry Concerns, for example, sponsors International Respect for Chickens Day . . .) In the section on the benefits of keeping chickens, the first item the booklet lists is garden health: "Chickens are perfect for the garden—they love to weed, get rid of pests, till your soil and make your soil richer." Neophyte I may have been, but my suspicions were immediately raised by the word "weed." Since when—and where—did chickens learn to distinguish between weeds and expensive, coddled ornamentals? In the gardening world, normally calm people can come to blows over arguments about what counts as a weed (especially true in any talk of native plants), so how did chicken brains sort it all out so effortlessly? Would they really munch on thistles but leave the culver's root intact?

Quickly I realized that the booklet writers' enthusiasm for their feathered friends had clouded their vision. I hightailed it to the hardware store and returned home with 25 feet of green plastic fencing. My Feathered Land Sharks could have the back half of the garden, but I was keeping the rest.

Not so fast, buster. After about a month of clear-cutting their back-half enclosure, the girls noticed that nothing was easier than hopping over wobbly 2-foot-high plastic fencing. I tired of the daily chase and roundup, and replaced the fence with a 3-foot-high number. That lasted for another couple of weeks, but soon enough they were flying over that, too. I cringed every time I looked out the kitchen window, wondering where the girls would be now. So, up went the 5-foot-tall plastic fencing. Since a gate was beyond my construction capabilities, I had to climb up two strategically placed stools, finessing a high jumper's twirl at the top, just to feed the girls. I was willing to put up with the inconvenience but Nog wasn't. Apparently she's a bionic chicken, and one day she managed to make it over the 5-foot fence. I was away when she did it, but I suspect that she launched her flight from the top of the coop, which was positioned near the fence. When I returned home to the AWOL creature, I felt utterly defeated. I just couldn't face a future of chasing chickens. Time to call in the troops. I must have been silently broadcasting panic pheromones to friends because within minutes of my escaped-Nog discovery, I received a phone message from two lifesavers, Nancy and Jane, saying that there was nothing they'd rather do the following night than come over and build me a gate, move the coop away from the fence, and extend the fence to the stratosphere. I was in luck. The chickens were in luck. My

193

neighbors' egg consumption was in luck. I banished all thoughts of exiling the gals to a farm.

The main lesson I learned through all of this wrangling was: don't believe what you hear about chickens being dumb. They are crafty creatures with an unstoppably curious urge to explore. Plan accordingly.

And plan to be surprised at every turn. Chickens rarely do what's expected. Mine certainly didn't, not in the "secured perimeter" idea or in the food department. But I shouldn't have been surprised. All of my pets have eating disorders. (My cat Joey eats vegetables by the pound—asparagus, Brussels sprouts, peas, edamame, spinach, olives, hot peppers, corn—while my other cat, Harold, eats little more than cheese—very expensive French cheese, unpasteurized please.)

Given what goes on in my household, I shouldn't have been surprised when my chickens defied all culinary rules at first. Hermione, Nog, and Roo entered this menagerie with firm plans to confound chicken convention. Sure, they ate the chicken feed (called "layers mash"—how unappetizing does *that* sound for breakfast?), but for those first few weeks they rejected all treats. Shredded apples, grapes, grass clippings scavenged from neighbors, the girls were having none of it. Even the cob of corn that I dangled with string from the wire covering the coop, both as toy and as snack, just swung in the breeze, a desultory testament to yet another species' eating disorder in my backyard.

Success, though, came in the form of organic cherries, purchased out of season at great expense and prepared with great effort. I pitted and chopped and contemplated peeling them. I placed the red-stained bowl in the chicken coop and watched my hens' finickiness turn to frenzy. Their heads bobbed at a great rate—if only they had lips they would have smacked them. The

194

hollow *tock, tock, tock* of their beaks hitting ceramic was percussive music to my ears. My girls had found their appetite and their true chicken nature. There was no turning back.

Now, my days are punctuated by food fun in the backyard. I recognize the irony of my behavior. Many people see chickens as a way to get rid of food scraps; I, on the other hand, actually buy fruits, vegetables, and special grains for the girls. My chickens are not waddling composters on legs; they're an excuse for exotic food purchases. Flax, quinoa, and strawberries—I scatter the seeds, grain, and berries in the dirt and am amused (for about the minute the whole race takes) as the girls run every which way in frantic feeding. The best part is the way that their legs and feet fling out from their sides like those of speed skaters.

In grade school we had a name for what I've become: a chocolate-bar friend. I suspect that my chickens see me as little more than a dependable source of snacks, but I'm okay with that. They, after all, are the dependable source of my newly egg-filled diet.

I may be biased, of course, but these are the best damn eggs I've ever had: firm, not runny, and full of gloriously rich flavor. And I don't think my friends are humoring me when they say the same thing. I positively beam when my neighbors hint for egg gifts, happy to spread the delicious wealth around. Big, fresh, glowingly yellow-centered eggs—and I am as proud of each one as if I'd popped it myself.

Another cautionary note, this one about the economic argument for keeping chickens in the city. There's no doubt that eggs from the backyard can be cheaper than eggs from the store or market, and there's also no doubt that in any carbon-emissions accounting, backyard eggs win hands down. But I have spent a fortune on my chickens. In my haste to set up my egg operation, there was no time for economizing. I bought a deluxe prefab coop

› Chicken-keeping Basics

PEOPLE WHO raise backyard chickens tend to be a chatty bunch, which means that there are all kinds of discussion groups on the internet. (There's even the equivalent of reality TV: tune in to hencam.com for live webcasting of a chicken coop in a backyard near Boston.) Of course, you may find that all this information is contradictory, but that's not only the nature of the internet commons, it's also the nature of urban chicken-keeping: what works in one place, what works with one particular breed, might not necessarily work for you. In the meantime, here are some tips:

> Chickens aren't space hogs, but they do require room: count on approximately 2 square feet of space per chicken in the shelter, and double that if you're not providing an area for free ranging.

> In order to lay well-formed eggs with hard shells, hens need a balanced diet with adequate calcium. The best way to supply this is through layers mash, which can be purchased at feed lots, or, in those cities with a strong chicken-keeping tradition such as Portland, Oregon, at pet stores. My hens eat approximately 1 cup of layers mash each per day. I keep the gals' feed dish topped up at all times, moving the food at the bottom to the top every day or two, to keep it fresh.

> Feeding your hens food scraps to supplement the mash is a great idea. Toss them leftovers, and you'll discover quickly what your hens prefer or eschew. For example, my gals aren't much interested in cabbage but they go crazy for salad greens. They also love most fruits and grains, and adore cheese and pasta. However, it's important not to go overboard in the food scraps department. If the chickens fill up on scraps, they may not eat enough of their mash, which can lead to brittle egg shells due to insufficient calcium intake.

> Feeding your hens egg shells can provide them with calcium, but be sure to first grind the shells as finely as you can. There's ominous talk in

discussion groups of chickens developing a taste for eggs, definitely not something you want to encourage. Fighting them for the eggs wouldn't be any fun at all.

> Chickens are omnivores and love meat and fish, though some people have found that too much fish affects the flavor of the eggs—fishily.

> Chickens don't have teeth. Rather, they grind their food in their gizzards, using small bits of grit that they consume. If you're feeding your hens layers mash, they'll get the grit they require. But if you're feeding them a diet high in kitchen scraps, be sure to supplement with purchased grit.

> Provide a soft bedding material for the nesting area where chickens lay their eggs. Wood shavings work well, but avoid sawdust and cedar shavings, both of which can irritate chickens' lungs.

> Fresh water is important. Make sure you keep their water dish full and change it daily. In winter, you may need to either buy a heated dish that keeps the water from freezing or change it more often.

> Chickens generate a lot of heat with their own bodies. However, in some parts of the U.S. and Canada, winter protection may be necessary. In prolonged periods of extreme cold, for example, their wattles and combs might get frostbitten. (Petroleum jelly smeared on the exposed bits helps prevent this.) Make sure they have dry bedding and a covered area (perhaps even insulated) where they can retreat from wind and snow. Some kind of heat lamp (a ceramic reptile light, for example) in the coop will provide sufficient additional warmth. According to the Society for Preservation of Poultry Antiquities, the following breeds are particularly well adapted to cold climates: Chanteclers, Wyandottes, Dominiques, Buckeyes, and Norwegian Jaerhons.

197

> For information on raising chickens for meat, get yourself a good source book such as *Raising Chickens for Dummies*.

designed in England and manufactured in the States—an Eglu made by a company called Omlet. The company trucked the coop from Ohio to Buffalo, and I borrowed a car to drive from Toronto to pick it up. There go my carbon credits.

Plus, I had to pay duty for this cross-border shopping excursion, adding to the cost, because while I could hide the coop in my backyard, there was no way I could hide the coop in the back of a Volvo. Smuggling was out. Anyway, it was all worth it for the conversation I had with the Customs fellow as I forked over my money.

"Anything to declare?"

"Yes, a chicken coop."

"A what?"

"A chicken coop."

"Does it come with chickens?"

"No."

"Good."

A few moments for the paperwork, then he said, "Hmm, this is the first chicken coop I've had declared today. Actually, this is the first chicken coop I've had declared ever."

For $84 in Customs fees, I made his day.

The Eglu was a luxury purchase, but one I justified to myself because it is designed to be city predator–proof. Since 2004, when the Omlet company launched the Eglu, more than 30,000 have been sold and given a test run by others. Good enough for my girls—I paid the high price so I wouldn't need to worry.

The only downside, other than the cost, is that I now have to endure occasional smirks from farmers, when I tell them about the Eglu. When I confess the price, I know that I am immediately relegated to the category of "city chick with more money than brains." The farmers I've talked with are much too kind to say so, but I see the looks on their faces.

Others more handy than me have rigged up ingenious coops for much less money. Online, you can view coops on wheels (so you can move your hens around the yard when they've eaten all the grass in one spot), coops in every conceivable size and shape, coops decorated with window box planters, coops with green roofs—there's no limit to the creative construction possible. If I were doing it again, at a more leisurely pace, I would get in touch with local farmers and see if any of them were willing to take on an urban coop commission. The most important thing is to make sure that the coop is Fort Knox secure, and I figure that a farmer-constructed model would be pretty safe on that score. (What I would emphatically not recommend is keeping chickens indoors—even though at least two companies sell chicken diapers for precisely this purpose.)

As for predators, I let the girls range freely during the day, and they haven't had any unfortunate encounters. Local cats perch on the top of the fence and peer down with intensely focused curiosity but seem to realize that those pointy beaks can do damage to felines. Mutual avoidance is their unspoken agreement. I'm convinced that my elderly cat, Harold, hasn't yet noticed the chickens, though my ginger troublemaker, Joey, spends a lot of his time thinking of ways to annoy them without sustaining injury. I don't have a dog and none have yet visited, but another Toronto chicken keeper sent me a photo of one of her girls standing on the back of her dog, both animals looking quite content.

Raccoons are more of a worry. I lock the girls in their coop at night to keep them safe, but in my neighborhood there is occasional raccoon activity during the day, around eight in the morning. Twice I have encountered raccoons when the girls were out of their coop, but so far they've just stared at each other and gone about their business. (I met someone who installed a baby monitor in his chicken run to keep tabs on the activity.)

199

The groundhog (what, I ask, is a groundhog doing in downtown Toronto?) avoids the chickens' enclosure, and the skunks are active only at night, when the girls are safe in their coop. The squirrels scurry around in the trees, doing damage to branches; they show no interest in the girls, nor do the girls in them. If I had opossums around or lived near a ravine with foxes, I'd have to completely enclose the chicken run with heavy-duty protection. But so far, there is peace, or at least a negotiated settlement, among the city creatures in my backyard.

THERE IS SOMETHING about keeping chickens that instantly transforms a solitary life into a social life. Never before have so many people hinted so broadly for invites or voiced outright requests to come over. From dear friends, to whom my door is always open, to passing acquaintances who clearly have a bold streak, the chicken-visiting petitions keep pouring in. I'm starting to feel like the popular girl in high school. The gals are a hit and I'm tagging along for the ride, happily serving as their event convener.

Managing this sudden influx of interest has led to a whole lot of soufflé parties at my house. I think of them as "meet, greet, and eat" events. One friend, who had come to a soufflé dinner early on in the series, overheard me arranging invites for another one, and he misheard the menu. "You're *eating* one of the girls?!" he sputtered. "Wow, the honeymoon didn't last long." No, I couldn't imagine roasting one of my birds, even when the inevitable happens and they each stop producing their six eggs per week. Though it varies among breeds and individuals, the average chicken starts laying at about six months old, is fertile for about three years, and can live for years longer. The math favors soup. But I figure my downtown coop will make a fine retirement village for menopausal hens. I may just be reaching that stage of life myself, and my plan to pamper the gals through "the change" will no doubt feel like a fiercely personal commitment. (However, if I ate much meat I would probably reconsider my seniors' housing for hens idea . . .)

In the meantime, though, it's soufflé for me and my friends. And deviled eggs by the dozen carted over to potlucks. And breakfast care-packages transported to my brothers by bus in another city. And egg gifts tucked into protective padding when I meet up with friends for coffee. It's a bit like perennial August around here and I'm the gardener with more zucchinis than I can possibly cope with—only there's a big difference. Friends' faces don't fall ("not another zucchini dirigible!") and outstretched hands don't snap back; there's not a hint of recoil when what's on offer are fresh eggs produced in a downtown yard that is so much like everyone else's and yet now so uniquely adorned.

I suspect that what my friends are savoring with each shared or gifted egg is the taste of chicken-keeping possibility. I may be imagining it, but in each murmured yum of appreciation for delicious flavor I hear a ruminative *um,* a hint of *"maybe I could do this, too?"* Then again, perhaps it's just my hope speaking, transferred to others. After all, if there's one thing a renegade urban chicken keeper loves, it's company.

It's been a year now, and my gals and I are settling in to our new lives. For the winter, I covered their coop and run in bubble wrap to keep out the wind and snow. One morning I discovered all three of the hens pecking away at the bubble wrap. They were popping holes in something that protected them. I hope I'm not doing the same thing in my own new life. But, then again, Leonard Cohen is right: the holes and cracks are where the light gets in.

ten

. . .

THE EDIBLE CITY

W HEN I CALLED my niece Deanna to hear all about her Christmas, she was especially excited about one present: a DS. I had no idea what that was and pressed for details. "I'm playing with it right now," she said. "It's for little games." And the game she was playing was called Gardening Mama. Apparently it involved moving "seeds" from a seed bag into the correct spot in the "garden," planting potatoes in the potato patch, sunflowers and strawberries throughout: "It tells you if a plant is wilting and needs some extra water. If you do it in less than thirty seconds, you get a gift. I won a garden bench and a hat!"

If an electronic game device is what it takes to spark a nascent interest in garden creation, I'm all for it. I'm cheered by the thought that Deanna might spend a little time during the winter moving potatoes around on the screen, and perhaps come spring she'll wonder about maybe planting some potatoes in the backyard.

Me, I'm wondering what it would be like to spend some time with my niece and nephew in a reimagined city—an edible city. I guess it's a bit like Deanna's DS: moving seeds around in the hopes that some will sprout and flourish. However wishful, this is what I envision:

It's a beautiful early September day and I'm on my way to pick up Deanna and Christopher from school. Walking down a path to the sidewalk, I pause to pinch the flowers off the basil in my small front-yard herb garden, so that the plants will grow bushier. It's been dry these past two weeks, but the herbs are fine—the rosemary, oregano, and tarragon haven't needed much care, though the basil required some extra watering. The scent in the air as my skirt brushes against the plants is heady and hunger-inducing. I make a mental note to stop by the local farmers' market, just down the street by the subway entrance, to pick up a snack. My neighbor's front-yard patch—vegetables mixed with more traditional ornamentals—has a bumper crop of tomatoes waiting to be picked. Maybe we'll trade: some basil for some tomatoes, so that we can both feast on caprese salad for dinner. And speaking of dinner, what should I choose from the backyard? The zucchinis are getting out of control. This morning there were two the size of footballs lurking under the leaves. It's time to eat them or grate them for the freezer. The green beans and potatoes are ready, too. With some hard-boiled eggs—made from fresh eggs collected yesterday from the hens at the community garden (it's my week in the chicken-care rotation)—they'd make a great Niçoise salad.

The late-afternoon heat hasn't yet begun to subside, but the shaded sidewalk offers protection from the sun. Branches from the boulevard fruit trees hang overhead. I can see that a couple of the cherry trees need pruning, and make a mental note to call the city's tree department tomorrow, to schedule a pruning appointment. I might even sign up for the course the city offers on fruit tree maintenance, so that I can finally shape the peach tree in my backyard and coax more fruit out of it. You can never have too many peaches. And then there are the serviceberries lining my street. Earlier in the summer, the tree nearest my house was loaded, almost sagging under the weight of the blue-black berry clusters, but the birds got there first and stripped the tree clean. Oh well, at least I was able to harvest lots of cherries with the volunteer group that gleans fruit from city trees. And, later in the fall, I could harvest apples with the same group from the trees in my neighbor Harold's yard—he's a bit too elderly for the ladder, but he's happy to direct the activity from his porch.

As I rush along the sidewalk, I almost don't notice my friend Steven hard at work on his hives. He'd asked the parks department for permission to set up some beehives in the pocket park that spans two side streets leading to the busy, main street. Most people—apart from the drug dealers—had avoided the park, but the hives changed all that. Now kids are always swarming around Steven as he works. They are full of questions, amazed that even though the bees land on his skin, they rarely sting. I'm glad that Christopher and Deanna are part of the local school group that he's training in the art of beekeeping—the group lessons count toward their credits in the urban agriculture and food literacy classes, which all students must now take during the school year.

Just a few more blocks to go. No time for a detour to the farmers' market in the parking lot of the subway station—it's crowded with late-afternoon commuters stocking up for dinner and I don't have time to stand in line. But the shopkeepers from the local business improvement association won't mind if I pick a cucumber from the vines planted in the street tree boxes and climbing up the trees' trunks. After all, there's a little note in each of the planters saying "Pick Me." Now there's a solution to the zucchini problem: a box in the boulevard with the extras. I'll add a "Please" to my "Take Me" sign and underline it for desperate emphasis.

The cucumber tastes good and has a satisfying crunch. But I'm relieved no kids see me eating it without having washed it first.

Rounding the corner, I can see Deanna and Christopher hard at work in the garden on the grounds of their school. Classes let out an hour ago, but the garden group has stayed late. Deanna seems to be handling the pitchfork like a pro. I think she's on compost-turning duty. The school has ten large bins, and a sign invites neighbors to drop off leftover food waste and garden clippings, so there's always lots of compost work to be done. Deanna and Christopher rush over and give me a slightly dirt-encrusted hug and start to enumerate the stories of the day: the slugs they squished in the morning, the raspberries they picked at lunch, the early fall lettuce planting they weeded on the green roof during recess. So many parents worked so hard to raise money for the rooftop garden, and the community now looks after it in the summer, before classes start. Deanna hands Christopher and me some carrots she has pulled from the ground. Washing the carrots at the outdoor tap, we begin to walk home, eating as we go.

The kids are game for a slightly different route, so we can walk past the Food Hub, the community center a few blocks away that, until a few years ago, had been a vacant lot. I want to pick up some pea seedlings from the community greenhouse there. The weather will be turning cooler soon and there's time for a second pea crop in the backyard. I'd also like to buy some of the pickles and preserves sold at the center, cooked up in the community kitchen. And there might just be some bread left from the outdoor bake oven. Deanna and Christopher won't be bored on this detour. They'll be busy feeding the fish in the aquaculture tanks.

The three of us walk toward the Food Hub, munching on carrots.

WHAT WOULD IT take for North American cities to be more welcoming of, and committed to, urban food production? What laws, regulations, attitudes, and social norms stand in the way of the edible city? And how can we harness this cultural moment of heightened food awareness to make changes that encourage more people to not only plant more food gardens but to embrace—and work toward—the pressing goal of fresh, healthy, affordable food available to all?

As the many examples in this book reveal, the latter goal often grows from the former: when we cultivate food, we cultivate communities and we cultivate a culture that values food as one of the most powerful connecting forces that exists between people. So, how are we doing, and, more importantly, how could we do better?

It is one of the great ironies of urban life that although food—its production, processing, storage, consumption, marketing, transportation, and waste management—impacts so much of our existence in cities, there is actually very little deliberate and conscious shaping of our cities *for* food. The planning profession—the people who shape the policies that guide virtually every aspect of urban development—and the engineering profession—the people who shape the infrastructure that delivers the services that make our cities tick—have, for decades, almost completely ignored issues related to food and the food system. Roads, housing, parks, zoning, water, transportation, waste, all are on the radar, but it is only relatively recently that food has explicitly entered the equation.

As just one example of the catch-up now required as a result of this oversight, consider compost. The lens through which cities have developed their compost programs is that of waste diversion. The engineering and policy goal, in other words, is to get organic materials out of landfills. What if the goal were, instead (or, indeed, as well), to produce a high-quality soil amendment that meets environmental standards for use in food production? This different goal would need to be considered in every aspect of how cities set up their composting systems, right from the beginning: from the materials accepted to ensure an uncontaminated product to the composting method employed. Without the food lens, the city might achieve its waste-diversion goals but the resulting compost could well represent a huge missed opportunity, unusable for the one purpose compost excels at—improving soil for the growing of food.

This is just one instance, and there are many others, of the way in which the frame directs the result. And for too long the frame has not included food.

When Kameshwari Pothukuchi and Jerome Kaufman surveyed urban planners in twenty-two U.S. communities, for an article published in the *Journal of the American Planning Association* in 2000, and asked them why they had such low levels of involvement in food system issues, two of the most common reasons given were that the food system is a rural issue, not an urban issue, and that the food system is not planners' "turf." Pothukuchi and Kaufman refer to this lack of involvement as a "conceptual hole," and itemize the numerous ways that the food system affects the economy, employment base, environment, and health of communities—everything from how people get to the grocery store to the impact of poor diet on health. "To be truly concerned about improving human settlements," they write, "planners need to incorporate food issues into their working models."

Perplexed by planners' disinterest in the food system, since the profession "claims to promote quality and livable settlements that meet basic needs and is concerned with connections between community systems," Pothukuchi and Kaufman conclude that "the food system is too important for planners to ignore." In an earlier, 1999 article, they suggest that cities could institute a "department of food."

Others have made similar suggestions. Betsy Donald, in her 2009 research report *From Kraft to Craft*, argues, for example, that

the province of Ontario needs a Ministry of Food: "not a ministry that focuses on agricultural commodities from a strictly rural
development perspective, but a ministry oriented toward food
from a health, ecological, social, cultural and economic perspective." Such a ministry would consider the food system "from field
to fork to waste"—in other words, it would take a holistic approach
to the multiple connections between food and everything from
land policies to transportation to energy use and climate change to
garbage management.

This vision of coordinated connecting-of-the-dots, of crossing
the boundaries that parcel out various aspects of the food system to
different provincial, state, and/or federal departments and jurisdictions, might be years away, but, in the meantime, there's promising
action at the local level. Many cities and municipalities in both
the U.S. and Canada have set up food policy councils, or similar
agencies, whose work involves taking precisely this holistic view
and recommending changes that would help lead to fresh, healthy,
affordable food available to all. They train the spotlight on that one
need from which all others flow—affordable access to good-qual-
ity, nutritious food—and on the ways that local governmental or
bureaucratic decisions either help or hinder the fulfilment of that
need. Basically, these food policy agencies are silo-busters.

Consider the example of the Hartford Food System, a nonprofit
organization. When interviewing people with low incomes about
the main causes of hunger in this Connecticut city, the group
found that poor access to transportation was a recurring theme.
People just couldn't get to the grocery store and were instead
shopping at convenience stores, where fresh, nutritious food is
often lacking. The group worked with the city to change its public
bus routes to ensure better access to supermarkets.

Access to land for the purposes of growing food is another key area that cities control and that their policies can help facilitate. Seattle's 2008 Comprehensive Plan, for example, includes "community gardening" as one of the goals for the use of the city's open space lands. (It's right there with other "active uses" such as "competitive sports" and "running.") San Francisco mayor Gavin Newsom ordered all departments—more silo-busting—to identify potential land that could be used for food gardens. Minneapolis mayor R.T. Rybak formed the Homegrown Minneapolis initiative in the summer of 2009 to encourage production and consumption of locally grown food by increasing the number of community, school, and backyard gardens. In Madison, Wisconsin, the 2007 Comprehensive Plan Update called for one community garden for every 2,000 households, and also created a new zoning district to allow for urban agriculture within the city. "What we wanted to do," says Rick Roll, a planner at the city of Madison, "was to make it easier for people to do things, rather than make them jump through hoops." Likewise, the San Diego Community Farms and Gardens Resolution committed the city to building more community gardens and farms.

In other words, change is happening, though it's true that the pace of city change can seem, at times, to be significantly less bold than public enthusiasm warrants. The city of Toronto, for example, has been a food policy leader (passing one of Canada's first municipal Food Charters in 2001), and is currently drafting an urban food strategy which, when completed and passed, will no doubt continue the city's visionary tradition in matters food-related. But even this forward-thinking, food-activist city can be surprisingly timid sometimes, such as when the committee drafting the plan requested, in February 2009, that the parks department "*consider* adding a pilot of edible planting in *one* of the City of Toronto's decorative planting areas." (Emphasis added.)

Surely we're ready, in cities throughout North America, for civic actions that ignite our imaginations and engage the possibilities far beyond things like a single pilot-project planter...

Here's a modest list, a start (and, of course, there are many other possibilities that people could and have come up with):

· Install community greenhouses in public parks, where people can grow seedlings for their yards and community garden plots.

· Provide municipally run soil-testing programs, for people to quickly, easily, and affordably determine the health of their soil.

· Post inventories of city-owned land available to the public for urban agriculture, to encourage people to "adopt" these spaces for food production.

· Institute regular "giveaway" days of city compost in parks— with full disclosure of compost test results.

· Establish city awards programs for front yard and boulevard food gardens.

· Create city-sponsored harvest parties at public parks, where people can bring produce to share and trade.

· Promote the idea of garden yard-sale days, where people with extra produce can set up tables in their front yards and sell (or give away) what they don't need.

· Provide horticultural desks in lobbies of city halls, where gardening groups can leave their literature and where gardening group volunteers can share information on food growing.

· Set up farmers' markets at city halls.

· Organize surprising and quirky municipal plantings—

pumpkins and watermelons, perhaps—on median strips or main
street boulevards.

• Design "adopt-a-planter" programs, encouraging volunteer growers to steward small food gardens in municipal decorative planter
boxes.

• Introduce orchard tree sale days, where people can buy affordable
fruit trees grown in city-run nurseries.

• Build city-sponsored apiaries in parks or at government buildings,
with the honey packaged and sold as a fundraiser for a good cause.

• Set up demonstration food gardens at city halls.

• Install demonstration rooftop food gardens at city facilities.

• Create children's food gardens in city parks.

• Facilitate community gardens in every city ward or district.
Consider locating them in unusual places—such as on police
department grounds (as they do at the Waterloo Regional Police
detachment in Hespeler, Ontario).

• Post public inventories of all edible fruit trees on city land, with
an invitation to harvest.

• Establish food preserving programs—pickling and jam-making,
for example—at city-run seniors' centers, where people who want
to learn the skill can be taught by those with the skill.

• Design city-produced maps of the city's "food shed," identifying
the locations of farmers' markets, stores that sell local produce,
community gardens, public edible landscapes, city fruit trees, and
nonprofit organizations, such as food banks and community food
organizations.

- Provide outdoor community bake ovens in public parks.

- Promote city-wide "grow-a-row" programs in which people are encouraged to grow extra produce for food agencies.

- Establish food gardens at all city-run social housing developments and community centers, with seed and plant fairs to encourage gardening.

- Provide subsidized compost bin programs for homeowners, renters, and apartment dwellers.

- Create city-run leasing programs for groups that want to do larger-scale food production on under-utilized land.

- Plant food gardens at every public school and public day care.

- Hire urban agriculture coordinators to work within city bureaucracies.

- Organize permit systems for vacant lots to be used for food production.

Unlike the top-down approach of many city programs, almost all of these proposals could be driven by community engagement. They offer the opportunity for cities to harness the food-focused energies that already exist. The city's role could be to facilitate rather than to direct; to encourage rather than to manage. Citizens could do the rest.

These suggestions might seem to avoid or ignore the deeper structural issues that stand in the way of wider-scale food production in cities—things like zoning rules that don't allow agricultural production in urban areas, a planning tradition that rigorously upholds a separation between agriculture and residential uses, or property-standards bylaws that mandate only conventional

213

landscaping such as grass and flower beds. While there's no doubt that these deeper issues need addressing (particularly the question of how we can incorporate farmland into urban design), this modest list of suggestions has a couple of things going for it. One, none of these items would be a huge drain on municipal resources. Two, they could be implemented relatively quickly and without necessitating cumbersome infrastructure changes.

But the biggest advantage of making these suggestions a reality is that they would announce—visibly, loudly, and clearly—that food growing *belongs* in our cities. They would celebrate and embrace the cultural shift happening all around us: the desire to be more connected with our food, the heightened interest in where our food comes from, how it is produced, who has (or does not have) access to it, and how we could make it available to all. They would put food in the front and center of our civic lives, where we can see it, grow it, taste it, and, most crucially, *know* it better.

THERE'S A MAN who sometimes stands at a busy commercial corner in downtown Toronto, at Bathurst and Bloor, asking for money. He's always cheerful in his petitions for spare coins. One summer day he was dressed in a Santa suit and his sign said, "The Sleigh Broke Down." The last time I saw him, his sign was even simpler: "Something is better than nothing."

There are few phrases I'd hang my hat on, but this is one. *Something is better than nothing.*

It seems to me that we are poised at the beginning of a growing movement ripe for cultivation. We've got a lot of something's that could make things better. And the instruments for change are some of the oldest tools we have in our kit: seeds, a little muscle, and a lot of hope and caring.

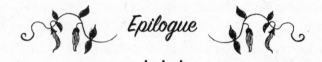

Epilogue

. . .

ADVENTURES IN POSSIBILITY

FROM THE PAUSE on the phone line, I could tell that I'd interrupted Robin in the middle of her lunch. She swallowed, and then—music to the ears of someone deep in the writing of a book about growing food in cities—said: "I'm just having some pasta with tomatoes from the parking lot." A parking lot garden might sound a bit odd, but months ago Robin had planted tomato seedlings in containers on the gravel parking pad in her back alley. These seedlings were now bearing fruit and providing lunch.

I like to think that tomatoes from the parking lot will soon be so common that we won't do mini-double-takes at the mental image. That the incongruity will fade. I feel much the same way about the phrase "city farmer." Conjoined but still carrying disjunction, maybe we just need to say it—and do it—often enough that the "city" qualifier hardly needs mention. That the idea of farming—anywhere, everywhere—will ease into our repertoire of urban behaviors so completely that we'll all share the "of course" of familiarity rather than surprise at an apparent oxymoron.

There are signs all around us that the idea of city farming is sneaking into popular consciousness, and the evidence points particularly to the younger crowd. I'm thinking of the pop star Pink, quoted in the *Toronto Star* in November 2008: "It's very punk rock to be out in a yard growing your own food." And you know that urban agriculture is moving mainstream when *GQ* magazine has a cover line asking, over the intent gaze of Zac Efron, "Have you discovered America's newest, tastiest (and damn cheap) food city?" The article inside, subtitled "A Man's Introduction to Gardening," includes this useful tip: "Gardening, like most hobbies worth doing, is best enjoyed with a beer." If any macho holdouts still harbor worries, *GQ* provides a list of gardening rules, the first of which is: "Gardening is not political. It does not make you countercultural, or an anarchist, or a Democrat. It's something for you to do for fun—and for tasty food." I may have my doubts about the politics line, but I'm all for people picking up trowels with their brews. In Britain, there's even an acronym for the demographic: Nyudies. New Yuppie Diggers.

Of course, we've had cultural moments of focus on urban food-growing before. The Depression, both world wars, and the 1970s stand out in particular. But I suspect that there's something different in the air now, something that will propel city farming with an energy that's got staying power. I'd locate the energy in a perfect storm of anxieties that many of us are keen to transform into something positive. Yes, there's bad news around every corner—our diets are implicated in epidemics of cancer, heart disease, and diabetes; our food system is poisoning the land, polluting the air, and depleting the soil; our collective will has still not figured out a way to ensure that everyone, everywhere has enough to eat—and yet this is also mobilizing so many to examine how we might chip away, in our own lives, at the problems taking us to the brink. We're finding at least one small corner of do-ability, one small corner of control over something that could hardly be more basic: the food we grow, the food we eat.

Roger Doiron of Kitchen Gardeners International calls this the transformation of gloom and doom into gloom and bloom: "I don't know if we'll solve the big international challenges, but I do know one thing: if we can get more people growing more of their own food, it will be part of the solution." And in that partial solution will be the full answer to a question more and more of us are asking: do we know where our food comes from?

When we grow it, we know.

So here's to reimagining our cities—and our place as citizens within them—as productive and generative.

Here, as a start, are ten ADVENTURES IN POSSIBILITY:

1. GROW SOMETHING—ANYTHING—SOMEWHERE—ANYWHERE. Start small if necessary. Simply plant something—even if it's just one thing—that's edible: in a container on your porch, balcony, or fire escape; in a window box; in a pot by your kitchen window; in the ground in the back or front yard of your house or apartment building; in a pot against an outside wall...Nurture your plants through a growing season and when they're ripe and ready to eat, thank yourself for making the effort and thank the sun, soil, and water for sustaining your effort. Consider any disappointments or outright failures as fodder for good stories, and opportunities to learn something. Rev up all your senses to high alert and eat the fruits of your labor with focused attention. Allow satisfaction and celebration to creep into each bite. Chew slowly, but plan quickly— for next year's growing season.

2. SCOUT SPACES, EAT THE VIEW. Whatever your living arrangement, take a look around at the land and the spaces that surround you and consider where you might

217

grow some (more) food. Could a corner of your lawn be given over to food production? Could your shrubs be edible and fruit-bearing as well as ornamental? Do you have room for a fruit tree or two? Could your flower bed include vegetables? Is there a local vacant lot that could be a food garden, a boulevard that could be planted?

3. SHARE WITH YOUR NEIGHBORS.
Grow an extra row for your local food bank or neighborhood social service agency. Grow yourself a reputation as a person of plenty. Share the bounty with friends, strangers, neighbors, and family (though you may want to think twice before off-loading your extra zucchini—some people consider this a hostile act). If and when you and your recipients reach inundation, consider preserving and pickling the excess for a later round of winter gifting.

4. SHAKE HANDS WITH A FARMER.
Truly, and as often as possible. Start at your local farmers' market. Talk with them about why they farm and what they grow and how they manage. Ask them how you can support what they do. (Hint: buy their food.) Find out what tips they might have for preparing their produce for the dinner table. When you know them well enough, escalate from shaking hands to hugs. And when you yourself are growing enough, try the label on for size: city farmer. It just might fit.

5. SEEK OUT GARDENERS.
Find the green thumbs in your community and ask them for help, for information, for seeds, for inspiration, for advice, for commiseration, for plant divisions, for tricks, for a shoulder to cry on if a plant dies, for a pat on the back when your seedlings sprout. Discover how they grow food in unusual ways and unlikely places. Do

not worry about imposing. Most gardeners carry an extra gene called "ready and willing." .

6. GARDEN WITH A YOUNGSTER.

Plant the seeds of a different, possible future with the next generation, who are the ones who will see it through. Introduce kids to the wonder and delight of nurturing growth. Hope that it becomes habit-forming.

7. ENLIST YOUR COMMUNITY.

Consider the places where you connect with your community and ask yourself (and them) if there are untapped growing opportunities in these social spaces. See if others share an interest in growing food and would like to do it with you. Start a garden where you can share the work, forge bonds, and harness opportunity.

8. JOIN A GROUP.

Chances are that a group of people who share your interest or passion (for whatever—weird fruits, compost, butterflies, heritage seeds, soil science) already exists. Seek them out, learn more. There's power, comfort, and camaraderie in numbers.

219

9. BE OPEN TO DOING THINGS DIFFERENTLY.

Consider the ways that the rules could be changed if the rules don't make sense. The new rules won't necessarily be easy, and they won't necessarily work, but conceiving of another way of doing things is the only way that things change for the better. (Warning: questioning the rules can lead to chickens.)

10. MAKE EATING WELL POSSIBLE—FOR EVERYONE.

In the end, this is what it comes down to, isn't it? That all people in our communities have enough good food to eat and enough opportunities and resources to make choices that are nourishing. We're not there yet. We've got a lot of growing to do.

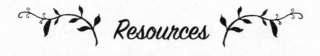

Resources

• • •

A SELECTED LIST OF URBAN FARMS
AND EDIBLE DEMONSTRATION GARDENS

ALONG WITH THIS highly selected list of demonstration farms
and gardens, there are thousands of community gardens in
North American cities. To find a community garden in your city,
contact the American Community Gardening Association. Some
cities also have community garden networks (for example, the
Toronto Community Garden Network).

CANADA
British Columbia
City Farmer (Vancouver): www.cityfarmer.info. Includes advice
on creating/installing a green roof, cob shed, organic food garden,
permeable lane, natural lawn, waterwise garden, worm and
backyard composter, and more.

Spring Ridge Commons (Victoria): http://lifecyclesproject.ca/
resources/bee_average/spring_ridge.php. Was a vacant gravel lot,
now is a productive growing space, including a bee garden.

UBC Farm (Vancouver): www.landfood.ubc.ca/ubcfarm.
Vancouver's last working farm, this 24-hectare teaching, research,
and community farm is located on UBC's Vancouver campus.

Alberta

University of Alberta Campus Community Garden (Edmonton):
www.su.ualberta.ca/services_and_businesses/services/
ecos/projects/garden. This organic garden features as many
sustainable agricultural practices as possible in order to showcase
environmentally friendly gardening techniques.

Manitoba

FortWhyte Farms (Winnipeg): www.fortwhyte.org. Engages
at-risk youth and provides them with the skills to increase their
economic and personal self-reliance using hands-on training in
innovative sustainable urban agriculture techniques.

Ontario

Black Creek Urban Farm (Toronto): http://trca.on.ca/near-
urban-agriculture/Toronto-urban-farm. Engages youth and the
community in urban organic farming, leadership development,
environmental stewardship, and health promotion.

FoodCycles at Parc Downsview Park (Toronto): http://foodcycles.
org. Vermicomposting project, urban food production, and
greenhouses.

Guelph Centre for Urban Organic Farming: www.organicag.
uoguelph.ca/learn/gcuof.html. A 1-hectare learning facility
established at the Arboretum of the University of Guelph to
complement the academic B.Sc.(Agr) Major in Organic Agriculture.

UNITED STATES

California

Center for Urban Agriculture at Fairview Gardens (Goleta): www.fairviewgardens.org. Small-scale urban food production, agricultural preservation, farm-based education, and community-supported agriculture (CSA) for Santa Barbara and Goleta.

City Slicker Farms (Oakland): www.cityslickerfarms.org. Increases food self-sufficiency in West Oakland by creating organic, sustainable, high-yield urban farms and backyard gardens.

Integral Urban House (Berkeley): Began in 1974 with the purchase and renovation of a large old Victorian house on a ⅛-acre city lot in Berkeley, showing urban residents how to become more self-reliant.

San Diego City College Urban Farm: www.sdcity.edu/esc/. One-third of an acre organic farm nestled in the heart of the city where students and community members work together to cultivate respect for the environment.

Soil Born Farms (Rancho Cordova): www.soilborn.org. Soil Born Farms allows youth and adults to rediscover and participate in a system of food production and distribution that promotes healthy living.

Colorado

Denver Urban Gardens: www.dug.org. Primarily serving low- to moderate-income populations in urban neighborhoods, DUG provides opportunities for participants to supplement their diet with produce grown in nearby public gardens.

223

Growing Gardens (Boulder): www.growinggardens.org.
Growing Gardens' mission is to enrich the lives of Boulder
County residents through environmentally sustainable gardening
programs that empower people to experience a direct and
deep connection with plants, the land, and each other.

District of Columbia
Common Good City Farm: www.commongoodcityfarm.org.
Common Good City Farm is an urban farm and education center
growing food for low-income residents in Washington, D.C.,
and providing educational opportunities for all people that
help increase food security, improve health, and contribute to
environmental sustainability.

Washington Youth Garden: www.washingtonyouthgarden.org.
This garden at the U.S. National Arboretum provides year-round
environmental science and food education for D.C. youth and
their families. The program teaches participants to explore their
relationships with food and the natural world.

Illinois
Grant Park Urban Agriculture Potager (Chicago):
www.growingpower.org/chicago_projects.htm. Two-thousand-
square-foot urban farm on Chicago's lakefront, adjacent to
Buckingham Fountain and Lincoln Memorial in Grant Park.

Jackson Park Urban Farm and Community Allotment Garden
(Chicago): www.growingpower.org/chicago_projects.htm. This
half-acre site is used as a community garden for local gardeners
and as a model urban farm, which Growing Power uses to
supply fresh produce to Chicago's south side.

Kansas

Kansas City Community Farm: www.kccua.org. The Kansas City Center for Urban Agriculture operates the Kansas City Community Farm (KCCF), a working, certified-organic vegetable farm.

Massachusetts

The Food Project (Boston): www.thefoodproject.org. Engages young people in personal and social change through sustainable agriculture. Works with more than 100 teens and thousands of volunteers to farm on 37 acres in eastern Massachusetts in the towns and cities of Beverly, Boston, Ipswich, Lincoln, and Lynn.

Nuestras Raíces Tierra de Oportunidades Project (Holyoke): www.nuestras-raices.org. A beginning farmer training project, new business incubator, environmental conservation and stewardship project, youth development initiative, and cultural development project, all by the Connecticut River in Holyoke.

Overlook Farm (Rutland): www.heifer.org. Experiential, hands-on, and interactive, Overlook is a working example of sustainable agriculture.

reVision Urban Farm (Boston): www.vpi.org/Re-VisionFarm/. The reVision Urban Agriculture Project works in conjunction with reVision House, a shelter for homeless young women and their children, located in the Franklin Field neighborhood of Dorchester. The urban farm is an innovative agriculture and aquaculture project aiming to increase access to affordable, nutritious, culturally appropriate food for shelter residents and community members through community-supported farm and greenhouses.

Michigan
Earthworks Urban Farm (Detroit): www.cskdetroit.org/EWG/.
Earthworks Urban Farm includes food growing and an apiary, with
a focus on social justice and knowing the origin of the food we eat.

New York
Queens County Farm Museum: www.queensfarm.org. Dating back
to 1697, the museum occupies New York City's largest remaining
tract of undisturbed farmland and is the only working historical
farm in the city. The farm encompasses a 47-acre parcel that is
the longest continuously farmed site in New York State.

Red Hook Community Farm (Brooklyn): www.added-value.org/
the-farms. A working farm where produce is grown, the farm
serves as the primary platform for youth empowerment programs
and farm-based learning work with school children.

The Vineyard (Rochester): The community garden and 2.69-acre
farm is on Rochester's only remaining agricultural land and it
serves as a cornerstone for neighborhood revitalization.

Oregon
The Urban Farm (Eugene): www.uoregon.edu/~ufarm/. A 1½-acre
garden/farm located at the University of Oregon. The Urban Farm
is an outdoor university classroom where students learn to grow
their own food organically and sustainably.

Zenger Farm (Portland): www.zengerfarm.org. A nonprofit farm
and wetland in outer southeast Portland dedicated to promoting
sustainable food systems, environmental stewardship, and local
economic development through a working urban farm.

Pennsylvania

Greensgrow (Philadelphia): www. greensgrow.org. Once a dilapidated industrial site, now an active, vibrant farm stand and nursery.

Mill Creek Farm (Philadelphia): www.millcreekurbanfarm.org. An educational urban farm dedicated to improving local access to fresh produce, building a healthy community and environment, and promoting a just and sustainable food system.

Texas

Urban Harvest (Houston): www.urbanharvest.org. A local charitable organization supporting a network of urban gardens, farms, and orchards. The gardens and farms are located at schools, youth centers, parks, housing projects, places of worship, vacant lots, and therapy centers, and serve to educate, strengthen community spirit, create therapeutic environments, and provide food and income.

Washington

Evergreen State College Organic Farm (Olympia): www.evergreen. edu/cell/organicfarm.htm. The Evergreen Organic Farm is close to an acre in size, and its produce is sold at a local farm stand. The farm's excess produce is given to the Thurston County Food Bank and local charities.

Wisconsin

Growing Power (Milwaukee): www.growingpower.org. Historic 2-acre farm is the last remaining farm and greenhouse operation in the city of Milwaukee. The urban farm includes six greenhouses, an aquaponics hoop house, an apiary, livestock, and extensive composting systems.

Troy Gardens (Madison): www.troygardens.org. On 31 acres of
urban property, Troy Gardens integrates mixed-income green-
built housing, community gardens, an organic farm, and restored
prairie and woodlands.

A SELECTED LIST OF URBAN AGRICULTURE
AND FOOD-RELATED ORGANIZATIONS

American Community Gardening Association:
www.communitygarden.org

BC Food System Network: http://fooddemocracy.org

Bronx Green-Up: www.nybg.org/green_up/

Canadian Organic Growers: www.cog.ca

Chicago Advocates for Urban Agriculture:
http://auachicago.wordpress.com

City Farmer: www.cityfarmer.info

Community Involved in Sustaining Agriculture:
http://buylocalfood.org

Detroit Agriculture Network: www.detroitagriculture.org

Detroit Black Community Food Security Network:
http://detroitblackfoodsecurity.org

FarmFolk/CityFolk: www.ffcf.bc.ca

Food Secure Canada: http://foodsecurecanada.org

The Garden Institute of B.C.: www.tgibc.org

Greencorps Chicago: greencorps@cityofchicago.org

Green Guerillas: www.greenguerillas.org

Greening of Detroit: www.greeningofdetroit.com

Growing Food and Justice Coalition:
www.growingfoodandjustice.org

Growing Gardens: www.growing-gardens.org

Growing Home: www.growinghomeinc.org

Growing Power: www.growingpower.org

Guelph Centre for Urban Organic Farming:
www.organicag.uoguelph.ca/learn/gcuof.html

Heifer Project International: www.heifer.org

Institute for Sustainable Horticulture: www.kwantlen.ca/ish.html

Just Food: www.justfood.org

LifeCycles Project Society: www.lifecyclesproject.ca

MetroAg: The Alliance for Urban Agriculture:
www.metroagalliance.org

Milwaukee Urban Agriculture Network: www.mkeurbanag.org

National Sustainable Agriculture Coalition:
http://sustainableagriculture.net

Neighborhood Gardens Association: www.ngalandtrust.org

NeighborSpace: http://neighbor-space.org

New York City Community Gardens Coalition: www.nyccgc.org

Oakland Based Urban Gardens: http://obugs.org/

Philadelphia Green: www.pennsylvaniahorticulturalsociety.org

Resource Centres on Urban Agriculture & Food Security: www.ruaf.org

San Francisco Garden Resource Organization: www.sfgro.org

Seattle Tilth: www.seattletilth.org

Seed Savers Network: www.seedsavers.net

Seeds of Diversity: www.seeds.ca

Slow Food: www.slowfood.com

Society for Preservation of Poultry Antiquities: www.feathersite.com/Poultry/SPPA/SPPA.html

Sustain Ontario: www.sustainontario.com

United Poultry Concerns: www.upc-online.org

Vancouver Community Agriculture Network: http://vcan.ca

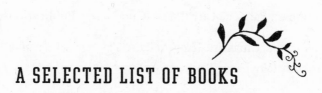

A SELECTED LIST OF BOOKS

BEES

Brackney, Susan. *Plan Bee: Everything You Ever Wanted to Know About the Hardest-Working Creatures on the Planet* (Hay House Publishers, 2010).

Buchmann, Stephen, and Gary Paul Nabhan. *The Forgotten Pollinators* (Island Press, 1997).

Conrad, Russ. *Natural Beekeeping* (Chelsea Green, 2007).

Flottum, Kim. *The Backyard Beekeeper: An Absolute Beginner's Guide to Keeping Bees in Your Yard and Garden* (Quarry Books, 2010).

Flottum, Kim, and Howland Blackiston. *Beekeeping For Dummies* (Wiley Publishing, 2009).

Ryde, Joanna. *Beekeeping: Self-Sufficiency* (Skyhorse Publishing, 2010).

CHICKENS

Damerow, Gail. *The Chicken Health Handbook* (Storey Publishing, 1994).

Damerow, Gail. *Storey's Guide to Raising Chickens* (Storey Publishing, 2010).

Daniel, Charles, and Page Smith. *The Chicken Book* (University of Georgia Press, 2000).

Foreman, Patricia. *City Chicks* (Good Earth Publications, 2009).

Heinrichs, Christine. *How to Raise Chickens: Everything You Need to Know* (Voyageur Press, 2007).

Lee, Andy. *Chicken Tractor: The Permaculture Guide to Happy Hens and Healthy Soil* (Chelsea Green, 1997).

Kilarski, Barbara. *Keep Chickens! Tending Small Flocks in Cities, Suburbs, and Other Small Spaces* (Storey Publishing, 2003).

Megyesi, Jennifer. *The Joy of Keeping Chickens: The Ultimate Guide to Raising Poultry for Fun or Profit* (Skyhorse Publishing, 2007).

Pangman, Judy. *Chicken Coops: 45 Building Plans for Housing Your Flock* (Storey Publishing, 2006).

Roberts, Michael. *Poultry House Construction* (Gold Cockerel Books, 1997).

Rossier, Jay. *Living With Chickens* (The Lyons Press, 2004).

Willis, Kimberley, with Rob Ludlow. *Raising Chickens for Dummies* (Wiley Publishing, 2009).

COMMUNITY GARDENS
Crouch, David, and Colin Ward. *The Allotment* (Faber and Faber, 1988).

Hou, Jeffrey, Julie Johnson, and Laura Lawson. *Greening Cities, Growing Communities: Learning from Seattle's Urban Community Gardens* (University of Washington Press, 2009).

Hynes, Patricia H. *A Patch of Eden: America's Inner-City Gardeners* (Chelsea Green, 1996).

Kirby, Ellen, and Elizabeth Peters, eds. *Community Gardening* (Brooklyn Botanic Garden, 2008).

Lawson, Laura J. *City Bountiful: A Century of Community Gardening in America* (University of California Press, 2005).

Naimark, Susan, ed. *A Handbook of Community Gardening* (Charles Scribner's Sons, 1982).

Nordahl, Darrin. *Public Produce: The New Urban Agriculture* (Island Press, 2009).

FORAGING
Brill, Steve, with Evelyn Dean. *Identifying and Harvesting Edible and Medicinal Plants in Wild (and Not So Wild) Places* (HarperCollins, 1994).

Peterson, Lee Allen. *A Field Guide to Edible Wild Plants: Eastern and Central North America* (Houghton Mifflin, 1999).

Thayer, Samuel. *The Forager's Harvest: A Guide to Identifying, Harvesting, and Preparing Edible Wild Plants* (Forager's Harvest Press, 2006).

GENERAL
Bittman, Mark. *Food Matters* (Simon & Schuster, 2009).

Cotler, Amy. *The Locavore Way: Discover and Enjoy the Pleasures of Locally Grown Food* (Storey Publishing, 2009).

Elton, Sarah. *Locavore: From Farmers' Fields to Rooftop Gardens, How Canadians Are Changing the Way We Eat* (HarperCollins, 2010).

Halweil, Brian. *Eat Here: Reclaiming Homegrown Pleasures in a Global Supermarket* (W.W. Norton & Co., 2004).

Henderson, Elizabeth. *Sharing the Harvest: A Guide to Community Supported Agriculture* (Nimbus Publishing, 1999).

Hough, Michael. *Cities and Natural Process* (Routledge, 2004).

Kingsolver, Barbara. *Animal, Vegetable, Miracle: A Year of Food Life* (HarperCollins, 2007).

Koc, Mustafa, et al., eds. *For Hunger-proof Cities: Sustainable Urban Food Systems* (IDRC Books, 1999).

Miller, Sally. *Edible Action: Food Activism and Alternative Economies* (Fernwood Publishing, 2008).

Mougeot, Luc. *Growing Better Cities: Urban Agriculture for Sustainable Development* (IDRC Books, 2006).

Mougeot, Luc. *Urban Food Production: Evolution, Official Support and Significance* (IDRC Books, 2000).

Nordahl, Darrin. *Public Produce: The New Urban Agriculture* (Island Press, 2009).

Palassio, Christina, and Alana Wilcox, eds. *The Edible City: Toronto's Food from Farm to Fork* (Coach House, 2009).

Pennington, Susan J. *Feast Your Eyes: The Unexpected Beauty of Vegetable Gardens* (University of California Press, 2002).

Petrini, Carlo, with Gigi Padovani. *Slow Food Revolution: A New Culture for Eating and Living* (Rizzoli, 2006).

Rempel, Sharon. *Demeter's Wheats: Growing Local Food and Community with Traditional Wisdom and Heritage Wheat* (Grassroots Solutions, 2008).

Roberts, Wayne. *The No-Nonsense Guide to World Food* (Between the Lines, 2008).

Steel, Carolyn. *Hungry City: How Food Shapes Our Lives* (Vintage, 2009).

GUERRILLA GARDENING
Borasi, Giovanna, and Mirko Zardini. *Action: What You Can Do With the City* (Canadian Centre for Architecture, 2008).

Reynolds, Richard. *On Guerrilla Gardening: A Handbook for Gardening Without Boundaries* (Bloomsbury, 2008).

Tracey, David. *Guerrilla Gardening: A Manualfesto* (New Society Publishers, 2007).

237

HOW-TO
Atha, Anthony. *Kitchen Gardens in Containers* (Collins & Brown, 2002).

Bartley, Jennifer. *Designing the New Kitchen Garden* (Timber, 2010).

Chase, Nan. *Eat Your Yard: Edible Trees, Shrubs, Vines, Herbs, and Flowers for Your Landscape* (Gibbs Smith, 2010).

Coleman, Eliot. *The Winter Harvest Handbook* (Chelsea Green, 2009).

Creasy, Rosalind. *Edible Landscaping* (Sierra Club/Counterpoint, 2010).

Day, Sonia. *The Urban Gardener* (Key Porter Books, 2003).

Dowding, Charles. *Salad Leaves for All Seasons: Organic Growing from Pot to Plot* (Green Books, 2008).

Gehring, Abigail R., ed. *Homesteading: A Back to Basics Guide to Growing Your Own Food, Canning, Keeping Chickens, Generating Your Own Energy, Crafting, Herbal Medicine, and More* (Skyhorse Publishing, 2009).

Guerra, Michael. *The Edible Container Garden: Growing Fresh Food in Small Spaces* (Gaia Books, 2000).

Hart, Rhonda Massingham. *The Dirt-Cheap Green Thumb* (Storey Publishing, 2009).

Hart, Robert. *Forest Farming: Cultivating an Edible Landscape* (Chelsea Green, 1996).

Hemenway, Toby. *Gaia's Garden: A Guide to Home-Scale Permaculture* (Chelsea Green, 2009).

Jacke, Dave, and Eric Toensmeier. *Edible Forest Gardens* (Chelsea Green, 2005).

Kourik, Robert. *Designing and Maintaining Your Edible Landscape Naturally* (Permanent Publications, 2005).

Lambertini, Ann, and Jacques Leenhardt. *Vertical Gardens: Bringing the City to Life* (Thames & Hudson, 2007).

Lanza, Patricia. *Lasagna Gardening for Small Spaces* (Rodale Books, 2001).

Larkcom, Joy. *Creative Vegetable Gardening* (Mitchell Beazley, 2006).

Mars, Ross, and Jenny Mars. *Getting Started in Permaculture: 50 Practical Projects to Build and Design Productive Gardens* (Permanent Publications, 2007).

Mollison, Bill. *Permaculture: A Designer's Manual* (Tagari Publications, 1997).

Pitzer, Sara. *Homegrown Whole Grains: Grow, Harvest, and Cook Wheat, Barley, Oats, Rice, Corn and More* (Storey Publishing, 2009).

Reich, Lee. *Landscaping With Fruit* (Storey Publishing, 2009).

Resh, Howard. *Hydroponic Food Production* (CRC Press, 2002).

Stout, Ruth. *How to Have a Green Thumb Without an Aching Back* (Fireside, 1990).

Trail, Gayla. *Grow Great Grub: Organic Food from Small Spaces* (Clarkson Potter, 2010).

Trail, Gayla. *You Grow Girl* (Fireside, 2005).

LAWNS

Flores, H.C. *Food Not Lawns: How to Turn Your Yard into a Garden and Your Neighborhood into a Community* (Chelsea Green, 2006).

Haeg, Fritz. *Edible Estates: Attack on the Front Lawn* (Metropolis Books, 2008).

Robbins, Paul. *Lawn People: How Grasses, Weeds, and Chemicals Make Us Who We Are* (Temple University Press, 2007).

POLICY/POLITICS/ACTIVISM

Blay-Palmer, Alison. *Food Fears: From Industrial to Sustainable Food Systems* (Ashgate, 2008).

Kneen, Brewster. *From Land to Mouth* (University of Toronto Press, 1989).

Nestle, Marion. *Food Politics* (University of California Press, 2007).

Nestle, Marion. *What to Eat* (North Point Press, 2007).

Patel, Raj. *Stuffed and Starved* (Melville House, 2008).

Pawlick, Thomas. *The End of Food: How the Food Industry Is Destroying Our Food Supply—and What You Can Do About It* (Greystone, 2006).

Redwood, Mark, ed. *Agriculture in Urban Planning: Generating Livelihoods and Food Security* (Earthscan Publications, 2008).

Schlosser, Eric. *Fast Food Nation* (Harper Perennial, 2005).

Smit, Jac, Annu Ratta, and Joe Nasr. *Urban Agriculture: Food, Jobs and Sustainable Cities* (United Nations Development Programme, 1996).

Viljoen, Andre. *Continuous Productive Urban Landscapes* (Architectural Press, 2005).

SCHOOL GROUNDS

Food and Agriculture Organization of the United Nations. *Setting Up and Running a School Garden* (FAO, 2006).

Waters, Alice. *Edible Schoolyards: A Universal Idea* (Chronicle Books, 2008).

URBAN FARMING

Ableman, Michael. *On Good Land: The Autobiography of an Urban Farm* (Chronicle Books, 1998).

Adams, Barbara Best. *Micro Eco-Farming* (New World Publishing, 2004).

Bartholomew, Mel. *All New Square Foot Gardening* (Cool Springs Press, 2006).

Carpenter, Novella. *Farm City* (Penguin Press, 2009).

Coyne, Kelly, and Erik Knutzen. *The Urban Homestead* (Process Media, 2008).

Damerow, Gail. *Barnyard in Your Backyard* (Storey Publishing, 2002).

Franceschini, Amy. *Victory Gardens 2007+* (Gallery 16 Editions, 2008).

Gibson, Eric. *Sell What You Sow* (New World Publishing, 1994).

Haakenson, Dan. *The Small Commercial Garden* (DakotaOak, 1998).

Houbein, Lolo. *One Magic Square: The Easy, Organic Way to Grow Your Own Food on Just Three Square Feet* (Experiment, 2010).

Jeavons, John. *How to Grow More Vegetables Than You Ever Thought Possible on Less Land Than You Can Imagine* (Ten Speed Press, 1982).

Logsdon, Gene. *Small-Scale Grain Raising* (Chelsea Green, 2009).

Madigan, Carleen, ed. *The Backyard Homestead* (Storey Publishing, 2009).

Olson, Michael. *MetroFarm: The Guide to Growing for Big Profit on a Small Parcel of Land* (TS Books, 1994).

Peacock, Paul. *The Urban Farmer's Handbook* (The Good Life Press, 2008).

Ruppenthal, R.J. *Fresh Food From Small Spaces* (Chelsea Green, 2008).

ACKNOWLEDGMENTS

I AM IMMENSELY GRATEFUL to the many people who helped shape this adventure:

- Those who shared their stories with me and who are named in the book—with thanks for your pioneering work.

- The folks at Greystone, in particular Rob Sanders and Nancy Flight; Emiko Morita, Alison Cairns, and Corina Eberle; Susan Folkins, Pam Robertson, Susan Rana, and Lara Smith.

- My agent, Jackie Kaiser, for a fortuitous conversation that turned a percolating idea into a book proposal.

- My mentors in the chicken department, Darlene Litman, Marcia Stevers, and Mark Trealout.

- Those (unnamed in the book) who answered my questions and made suggestions: Amy Blankstein, Richard Brault, Sheila Burvill, Jodi Callan, Helen Cameron, Ted Cathcart, Kevin Cavenaugh, Joe Clement, Melanie Coates, Pleasance Crawford, Shannon Crossman, Topher Delaney, Craig Diserens, Peter Dorfman, Clara Kwon, Erin MacDonald, Madhu Mahadevan, Akiko Masutani, Kurt Metzger, Debbie Nolan, Maria Nunes, Steven Peck, Patrick Steiner, Owen Taylor, Victoria Taylor, Edwinna von Baeyer.

- The first readers, who so generously responded, suggested, supported: Nancy Chater, Jane Farrow, Dave Harvey, Eileen Leather, Robin Sarafinchan.

- Friends who offered advice, sustenance, and feedback: Michael Schellenberg (a brilliant, kind, and, when necessary, tough editor

who guided my pen and bolstered my spirits), Rob Firing, Chris
Nuttall-Smith, Carol Toller.

- Friends, colleagues, mentors, heroes whose work on urban agriculture, food, and gardening has inspired me: Martin Bailkey, Lauren
Baker, Deborah Barndt, Gwynne Basen, Dagmar Baur, Laura Berman, Stewart Chisholm, Cam Collyer, Pleasance Crawford, Debbie
Field, Michael Hough, Zora Ignjatovic, Seana Irvine, June Komisar,
Michael Levenston, Rod MacRae, Joe Nasr, Wayne Roberts, Nick
Saul, Lori Stahlbrand, Roberta Stimac, Rhonda Teitel-Payne,
Edwinna von Baeyer, Gerda Wekerle.

- For crucial research assistance: Cate Cochran, Brenda Ferguson,
James Kuhns, Tina Pittaway.

- For Lindsay Karabanow and her family, who opened their home,
garden, and stories to me.

- For dear friends who held my hand and helped my heart: Debbie
Adams, Julie Burnett, Jane Farrow, Peter Fleming, Chris Gittings,
Robin Sarafinchan.

- For Hermione, Nog, and Roo, cheerful companions on a path of
new possibilities; and for Harold (grey and glum) and Joey
(curious and orange).

- For my brothers, Keith and Ross, who offer love and support
through all, and my sister Eileen, whose love and support included
typing.

I started writing this book at an ending and finished it at a
beginning. For Andrew, with love.

INDEX

Abley, Mark, 16
Adams, Sam, 35
Added Value, 79
Advent Lutheran Church, 119–22
Afri-Can FoodBasket, 120
agriculture, 44–45, 49–50; industrial, 13
Alex Wilson Community Garden, 143–44
Allen, Erika, 112
Allen, Matt, 76–78
allotment gardens, 11; history of, 139–41
Alternatives, 104
American Community
    Gardening Association, 69, 144
Andrews, Asenath, 125–27
Animal, Vegetable, Miracle, 50
Artists' Gardens, 155–58

Backyard Bounty, 56–58
Backyard Homestead, The, 51
backyard sharing, 55–56, 58–65.
    See also Sharing Backyards
    Initiative; SPIN-Gardening
Bailkey, Martin, 69
balcony gardening, 93–95, 104–5, 217
Banks, Kerry, 103
bees, 40, 99, 100, 102–3, 104,
    128, 205, 212
Behrens, Matthew, 36
Bellows, Anne C., 49, 130
beneficial insects, 98. *See also* bees
Ben Nobleman Park, 136
Bittman, Mark, 24
Blooming Boulevards, 163
Bosnia, 149–52
boulevard gardening, 161–67, 211,
    217; legality of, 164; in Guelph
    162–63; in Minneapolis, 163, 166;
    in Vancouver, 162; tips for, 164–65
Brdanovic, Davorin, 151

Brick Works, 104
Brookings Institution, 81
Brown, Katherine, 49, 130
Burns, David, 174
Burnside Rocket Building, 98–99

Calgary Food Policy Council, 147
Calgary Liberated Urban
    Chicken Klub, 187
Cantaloupe Garden, 15
Catherine Ferguson Academy, 123–27
Center for Urban Agriculture, 87.
    See also Greensgrow
Chez Panisse, 123
Chicago, 69–71
Chicago Honey Co-op, 102, 104
chickens, 40, 179–201; concerns about,
    182–88, 188–89, 190, 199–200;
    coops, 195, 198–99; and food,
    194–95, 196–97; and gardens,
    191–94; how to raise, 191–97;
    laws about, 182, 184, 185–87, 188
Chicken Underground, The, 185
children's gardens, 124, 212, 219.
    See also school gardens
Christensen, Roxanne, 55
church gardens, 37, 119–22
Cities and Natural Process, 40
Cities Feeding People Report 8, 146
City Chicken Guide, The, 192
City Chicks, 187
City Farm, 70–71, 82
City Farm Boy, 55, 98
City Farmer, 67
City Farmer Newspaper, 103
city farming: attitudes toward, 6–7,
    11–12, 41–44, 45–46, 48; benefits
    of, 12–14, 16–20, 28, 29–30, 128–30;
    front yards, 107–14; history of, 5,

245

41–44, 45, 216; liability, 84–85;
opportunities, 12, 67–68; statistics
about, 48–50, 51–54, 55, 67–68, 86;
tax incentives, 81, 84; yields,
47–54, 55; 67–68, 86. *See also* bees;
chickens; soil; SPIN-Gardening;
Victory Gardens
City Improvement League of Montreal, 88
Clinton Community Garden, 142
Collingwood Neighbourhood
House, 100, 173
Collyer, Cam, 122–23
Committee for the Cultivation
of Vacant Lots, 88
Community Food Security
Coalition, 49, 130
community gardens, 35, 46, 81, 84, 116,
119–22, 128, 131–53, 210, 212; allotment gardens, 139–41; Bosnian,
148–52; connection with health,
128–30, 147, 148; Montreal, 144–46;
municipal support of, 139–41, 144–48,
210; New York, 142; starting, 145;
statistics about, 142, 144, 146, 147;
Toronto, 147–48; types of, 138;
vandalism of, 131–32
Community Gardens Association
of Toronto, 40
community greenhouses, 206, 211
community kitchens, 100, 206
community orchards, 136–38
Community Shared Agriculture, 56, 79
*Complete Home Landscaping and
Garden Guide*, 109
compost, 20, 43, 79, 82–83, 95, 105,
114–18, 127–28, 164, 206, 207–8;
vermicomposting, 83, 116–17
Conboy, Fred, 39
container gardening, 47–48,
94–95, 104–5, 217
Corboy, Mary Seton, 85–88.
See also Greensgrow
Counter, Douglas, 162
Creasy, Rosalind, 110–11

Curran, Liz, 61–62
Cuyahoga County Planning
Commission, 81

Dale, Fred, 58
Daly, Herman, 44
dandelion wine, 171
Davie Village Community Garden, 84
Dervaes family, 52
Despommier, Dickson, 106
Detroit: Catherine Ferguson Academy,
123–27; farming in, 72–78; Hantz
Farms, 76–78; vacant land in, 68–69
Detroit Agriculture Network, 74
Detroit Black Community
Food Security Network, 74, 77
Detroit Collaborative Design Center, 74
Detroit Food Policy Council, 74
Dhalwala, Meeru, 140
Dixon, Sheila, 35
Doiron, Roger, 34, 35, 217
Donald, Betsy, 208–9
Downsview Park, 116
Dunn, Ken, 71

Eat Here, 5
edible landscaping, 110–114,
166–67, 204, 211–12
edible native plants, 174, 175
Edible Schoolyard, 123
edible weeds, 171, 176
Efron, Zac, 216
End of Food, The, 13
Environmental Building News, 97
Environmental Youth Alliance, 97, 102
Evergreen, 122, 123

Fair Food Network, 76
Fairmont Royal York Hotel, 98–100
Fallen Fruit, 174
Farm-A-Lot, 75
farmers' markets, 13, 35, 126, 204, 211, 218
Field, Debbie, 44, 127–28
Fischer, Beatrice, 58

Food and Agriculture
    Organization (FAO), 49
FoodCycles, 116–18
food gardens: aesthetics of, 28;
    attitudes toward, 6, 9–11,
    42–44; cost, 54; maximizing
    space in, 53; shade, 64; symbolic
    locations, 32–36, 212, 213; unlikely
    places, 92–93, 106–7; yields, 47
Food Matters, 24
food miles, 4–6, 20–25
food policy councils, 209
FoodShare, 23, 44, 127, 128
food sovereignty, 24
food system, 4–6, 13, 44–45
Forage Oakland, 176
foraging, 168–77; guidelines for, 173
Foreman, Patricia, 187
Frances Beavis Community Garden, 52
Fresh Food from Small Spaces, 51
From Kraft to Craft, 208–9
front yard gardening, 107–14, 211, 217
fruit-tree gleaning, 137, 174–77

Garcelon, David, 99–100
Garden Resource Program
    Collaborative, 74, 76
Gary Comer Youth Center, 101
Gibbons, Euell, 33
Giuliani, Rudolph, 142
Gould, Adrian, 15
GQ magazine, 216
Granger, Ben, 95–96
Grant Park, 112
Graykowski, Scott, 163, 166
Greater Vancouver Regional District, 49
Green Guerillas, 159, 160
greenhouse gas emissions, 21–24
Greening of Detroit, 74
Green Living Technologies, 96, 97
Greensgrow, 86–88
Green Streets, 162
Growing for Green, 136
Growing Gardens, 184

Growing Green, 80
*Growing Healthy Food on
    Canada's School Grounds*, 123
Growing Power, 112
Growing Together, 94–95
Guelph Boulevard Club, 162
Guelph Environment Network, 163
guerrilla gardening, 155–61;
    history of, 159–60;
    and seed bombs, 160
Guerrilla Gardening: A Manualfesto, 159

Halweil, Brian, 5
Hanavan, Louise, 185–86
Hantz Farms. *See* Detroit
Harfleet, Paul, 160
Hartford Food System, 209
Hautecoeur, Ismael, 93, 104
Hawkins, Christopher, 59–60
*Health Benefits of Urban
    Agriculture*, 49
Hincks-Dellcrest Centre, 94
Hmong Community Garden, 142
HomeGrown, 52
Homegrown Minneapolis, 210
Horst, Megan, 80
Hough, Michael, 40
Howard, Manny, 52
Hutchinson, Tom, 101
Huterer, Julia, 150
Hutton, Rebekka, 117

Ignjatovic, Zora, 150
imported food, 16–17, 25–30, 44–45
"Incredible Edible House," 106
Institute for Innovations in
    Local Farming, 55
International Development
    Research Centre, 146

Johnson, Betsy, 144
Johnson, Boris, 147
*Journal of Nutrition Education
    and Behavior*, 129

Journal of the American Planning Association, 208
Just Food, 184–85, 192

Kastner, Erin, 176
Kaufman, Jerry (Jerome), 69, 208
Keep Chickens!, 184
Kensington Market, 2–3
Kilarski, Barbara, 184
Kingsolver, Barbara, 50–51
Kitchen Gardeners International, 34, 217
Kliewer, Karin, 174–75
Korbobo, Raymond, 110
Kropla, Bob, 56
Kuhn, Monica, 97–98

Lam, Sunny, 117–18
Landscape Architecture Review, 89
Langley-Turnbaugh, Samantha, 19
lawn, 42, 107–10, 218; aesthetics of, 108; conversion to vegetable garden, 43; history of, 42; statistics about, 107–8
Lawn People, 108
lead contamination, 18–19, 31–32, 52, 85
Leopold Center for Sustainable Agriculture, 24
Levenston, Michael, 67–68
LifeCycles Project Society, 59
Lincoln Institute of Land Policy, 69
Little City Farm, 174–75
Liz Christy Community Garden, 159
local food, 22–24, 28, 44
Lololi, Anan, 120
Lucretia, Lara, 94–95

MacKinnon, J.B., 25
Macoun, W.T., 89
Mad City Chickens, 185
Madigan, Carleen, 51
maple-tree tapping, 169
Marvy, Ian, 79
McCormack, Gail, 163
McNeill, George, 99
MetroFarm, 49

Mills, Pastor Mike, 119–22
Milwaukee, 69
Montreal Melon, 15–16
Moore Landscapes Inc., 112
Multicultural Association of Bosnian Seniors and their Friends, 150

National Gardening Association, 54, 144
National Park Service, 31
National Society of Allotment and Leisure Gardeners, 141
National War Garden Commission, 38
Neighborhood Urban Agriculture Coalition, 87
NeighborSpace, 84
Neuzil, Mark, 36
New Horizons Community Garden, 149–52
Newman, Will, 19
Newsom, Gavin, 210
New York Restoration Project, 142
North American Initiative on Urban Agriculture, 130. *See also* Community Food Security Coalition
Not Far From The Tree, 137, 177
NOW magazine, 36, 44
nutrition, 14, 28, 122, 128–29, 148, 209

Obama, Michelle, 31–32, 35
Ohrt, Russ, 113–14
Olson, Michael, 49
O'Malley, Katie, 35
Omnivore's Dilemma, The, 33
100-Mile Diet, The, 25
On Guerrilla Gardening, 159
Ontario Hydro Horticultural Club, 40
Oregon Sustainable Agriculture Land Trust, 19
Ottawa Horticultural Society, 89

Pagliarulo, Marco, 104–5
Paignton Zoo, 97
Pawlick, Thomas, 13, 14
People's Garden, The, 32

Philadelphia, 55, 68, 69, 85, 88, 129
Philadelphia Urban Gardening
    Project, 129
phytoremediation, 19
pigs, 40
Pingree's Potato Patches, 75
Pink, 216
Pirapakaran, Nandiny, 94–95
Pitera, Dan, 69, 74
Poe, Edgar Allen, 71
policies, 206–14
Pollan, Michael, 33
PollutionWatch, 85
potager, 111–12
P-Patches, 80–81
Prima Properties Ltd., 81
Pothukuchi, Kameshwari, 208
Progressive Policy Institute, 17

Quayle, Moura, 81, 89

raised beds, 18, 86
real food: conscious consumption
    of, 14, 29; and seasonality, 4, 27–29
Recipe for Change, 128
Red Hook Community Farm, 79–80, 82
Region of Waterloo Public Health, 22, 44
Reinsborough, Laura, 177
Reiss, Vivian, 166–67
Relief Gardens for the Unemployed, 89
*Report on Community Gardening
    in Canada,* 81
Resource Center, 70, 71
ReVision Urban Farm, 96
Reynolds, Richard, 159
Richler, Noah, 25
Richmond Fruit Tree Sharing Project, 176
Rios Clementi Hale Studios, 106
Robbins, Paul, 108
Roberts, Greg, 174–75
Roberts, Wayne, 21, 147
Robertson, Gregor, 35
Roll, Rick, 210
rooftop gardening, 91–96, 97–101,
    102, 212; low-tech method, 91–92

Rubinstein, Helena, 37
Ruppenthal, R.J., 51
Rybak, R.T., 210

San Diego Community Farms
    and Garden Resolution, 210
Satzewich, Wally, 55
school gardens, 122–28
Science Barge, 106
Score, Michael, 76
seasonality, 27–29
Seasoned Spoon Café, 101
Seattle Tilth, 184
Sereduk, Tom, 85. *See also* Greensgrow
shade gardening, 53, 64
Sharing Backyards Initiative, 59
sheet mulching, 43
Shriver, Maria, 35
Shuman, Michael H., 76
Sky Vegetables, 99
skyscraper farms, 106–7
Small-Mart Revolution, The, 76
Smit, Jac, 49, 130
Smith, Alisa, 25
Smith, Marian, 120, 121
Snow, Jean, 56
Society for Preservation of
    Poultry Antiquities, 197
Society of Environmental Journalists, 36
soil: contamination of, 16–20, 52, 85–86;
    testing of, 17–20, 31–32, 211
Somerton Tanks Demonstration Farm, 55
SPIN-Gardening, 54–58
Stalking the Wild Asparagus, 33
Stirling, Shannon Lee, 56–58
St. James Town, 94–95
Stop Community Food Centre, 60.
    See also Yes In My Back Yard
Streets Are For People, 3

Tall Gallery, 109
Taylor, Dave, 105–6
Taylor, Ken, 16
Taylor, Lee, 15
Tesco, 21

Teulon, Ward, 55–56, 98
Thompson, Michael, 102–3
Thoreau, Chris, 52
Tom Riley Park, 150
Toronto Action for Social Change, 36
Toronto Balconies Bloom, 95
Toronto Beekeepers Co-operative, 99
Toronto Environment Office, 147
Toronto Food Policy Council, 147
Toronto Public Space Committee, 160
Toronto Star, 25, 58, 216
Toronto Urban Growers, 58
Toronto Vacant Lots Cultivation
    Association, 88
Tracey, David, 159
Trail, Gayla, 108
Trust for Public Land, 142
Turner, Chris, 109

Uncommon Ground restaurant, 100
United Nations Food and Agriculture
    Organization, 21
United States Department of Food
    and Agriculture (USDA), 14, 32, 38
Université du Québec à
    Montréal (UQAM), 101
urban agriculture, 5, 41, 48–51, 70–71,
    229–31. See also city farming;
    Detroit; Greensgrow; Neighborhood
    Urban Agriculture Coalition
    (NUAC); vacant land
Urban Farming, 74, 96
Urban Farming Food Chain, 96
urban planning, 207–10

vacant land, 69–89, 213
Vacant Land in Cities, 81
Vacant Lot Association, 89
Vacant Lots Garden Club, 89
Vancouver Convention Centre, 102
Vancouver Fruit Tree Project, 176
Vancouver Park Board, 146–47
Vancouver Public Space Network, 84
Vandersteen, Gail, 55

VanGrow, 140
Vertical Farm Project, 106
vertical landscaping, 86
Victory Gardens, 32, 34, 37–41;
    British campaigns, 40–41; Eleanor
    Roosevelt, 32; World War I, 37–38;
    World War II, 32, 37, 38–40
Village Harvest, 176
Vilsack, Tom, 32–33
Vincent Callebaut Architectures, 106

Wadud, Asiya, 176
Waterloo Hen Association, 186
Waterloo Regional Police, 212
Waters, Alice, 123
Weertz, Paul, 125–27
White House food garden, 31–35, 54;
    Eat the View campaign, 34; history
    of, 33. See also Obama, Michelle
Wilson, Tim, 71
Wood, Henrietta, 89
Woodsworth, Bob, 67

Xuereb, Marc, 22

Yakini, Malik, 77–78
Yes In My Back Yard, 60–63
Young, Coleman A., 75
YWCA, 100

Zakonovic, Miodrag, 149
zoning laws, 146, 207, 213–14